WEST BUCKLAND SCHOOL
— SCHOOL —

Berwick Coates

HALSGROVE

First Published in Great Britain in 2000 by Halsgrove

British Library Cataloguing in Publication Data

Data for this publication is available from the British Library

ISBN 1 84114 080 5

HALSGROVE

Halsgrove House
Lower Moor Way
Tiverton
Devon EX16 6SS
Tel: 01884 243242
Fax 01884 243325
www.halsgrove.com

Printed and bound in Great Britain by
Hackman Printers Ltd, Rhondda

CONTENTS

ACKNOWLEDGEMENTS

Very few authors produce a book with absolutely no help whatever. I am not one of them.

I am grateful to West Buckland School for allowing me to use the resources of its Archive for the purposes of this book, and to its Headmaster, John Vick, for his interest and encouragement.

The West Buckland Masonic Lodge, and particularly its Treasurer, Colin Byfleet, have given support, especially in the vital area of finance. I thank them too.

My wife has listened to practically every item of the book, fresh from the oven, as you might say – like bread, with all its woolliness and holes.

I am indebted to my publisher, Steven Pugsley, for his promptness and efficiency. Anyone who has not experienced them has no idea of the extent of his powers of advocacy and persuasion.

Finally, I should like to express my debt to my colleague, Stephen Prior, who spent a long time at the end of a busy term scanning and preparing the photographs for the press. Without his help, I could never have met the deadline.

I must make it clear that no interested authority connected with West Buckland School has made any attempt to influence what I have written. There is no attempt in this book at a party line, an official version, a public statement. Whatever has been said here represents my view of things, and my view only. Any mistakes, therefore, are mine. Any offence, should any have been given (and I have striven hard not to do so), is also my responsibility.

Berwick Coates

◨ WITHOUT ROOTS, NOTHING GROWS ◨

How long have you lived in your present house? Ten years? Twenty? And how many people live there? Four? Five? Say six, with the cat. Think how much material you have accumulated about the past of that house and its six inhabitants in those ten or twenty years. And how interesting it is when you come across it. Have you ever crouched for hours over a dusty trunk in the attic when you went up there in the first place to fix a broken tile? Exactly.

Now – imagine a building with nearly 150 years of continuous occupation by over 5000 people – and with scores of cupboards, drawers, attics, nooks and crannies.

So a school archive should have a lot to tell, if you can prise open its secrets. All you need is a little patience, a dash of imagination, and a willingness to see that there is often more than one side to the truth. And with the initials B.C., what better qualifications could I have?

I also have a swish new office, with a most discreet 'Archive' nameplate in Gothic script on the door. From the outside it looks a bit like a speakeasy. But, as with the speakeasy, do not be put off by the severe exterior; come and see what delights await you inside.

What is my aim? To make all those connected with the School (and anyone else for that matter) more aware of its past – and so of their own past. It is a very human desire to know more about where one comes from.

That is not to say that the Archive is trying to pull you back into the past. Knowledge and awareness of the past is not an end in itself; it is a means to an end. History is not the science of the dead; it is one of the arts of living. What matters, of course, is the present and the future. Any school wants its pupils to look ahead, to take the world by storm, to reach up to the stars. But knowing where they come from will help them to do that better. The past – and the Archive – represent a school's roots. Without roots, nothing grows.

The Old Library, set up by M. B. Snell (1866-1870).

◈ THE END AND THE BEGINNING ◈

In the summer of 1998, it became clear that I was coming to the end of my History teaching. The Headmaster wrote a letter to me to say that, as I was a part-timer, and because of the exigencies of the timetable, it would not be possible to offer me any more History teaching time. So that was that.

However, he came up with the idea of a School Archive, which he had been turning over in his mind for some months. Would I be interested in setting up such a department? (I am over-simplifying and condensing, but that, in effect, is what it amounted to.)

I said yes, I would. Delighted. Splendid idea. Super. Absolutely terrific. (Well, consider the alternative.)

It was rather like Henry Morton Stanley agreeing to take on his editor's assignment to go to Africa and find Livingstone. Neither of us knew anything about the subject; neither of us had the slightest idea of the implications of what we had just agreed to do. Stanley didn't know if Livingstone was even alive; I didn't know how much, if any, documentation of the past still survived. Livingstone could have been anywhere in Central Africa; my material could be anywhere across the whole campus.

Both of us were tempted and beguiled by our superiors with dazzling possibilities. Do you remember when Toad showed Ratty and Mole his gypsy caravan for the first time, and how he painted a beautiful picture of the wanderer's life? 'There's real life for you, embodied in that little cart. The open road, the dusty highway, the heath, the common, the hedgerows, the rolling downs! Camps, villages, towns, cities! Here today, up and off to somewhere else tomorrow! Travel, change, interest, excitement! The whole world before you, and a horizon that's always changing!'

Stanley's editor, Gordon Bennett, lured him with the chance of the greatest journalist scoop of the century; my Headmaster talked of private offices and data bases and press coverage and public relations and archive lessons and 'involvement' of practically everybody from the humblest junior to the oldest old boy. If the idea 'took off', it seemed only a matter of months before the Archive Department became a mixture of museum, clearing house, technological nerve-centre, P.R. bureau, and Piccadilly Circus.

Well, I don't know about Piccadilly Circus, but the Archive has certainly provided a whole world of fresh horizons to this ex-History teacher, many of which I would not have suspected.

The dust, the old photographs and the stained glazing, the frayed maps, the yellowing pages – all these were no surprise. The endless lists, the bound copies of minutes of old societies and boards and committees, the moth-eaten blazers and the tarnished cups – no surprise either.

No – I don't think it was what I found that was unexpected; it was where I went to get it and the people I met in the course of it.

Anyone who works in a large establishment soon wears little ruts in which his regular work takes him. If he is busy, or preoccupied, he does not take much notice of things on either side of those ruts. And he has little knowledge of other destinations to which his ruts do not take him.

So, as a History teacher, I knew about classrooms and corridors and libraries and lecture rooms. I knew little about the scores of other rooms. It was the same with faces.

Now – as the School Archivist, I go to all sorts of other places, and I see, regularly, all sorts of other people I barely knew before.

Take Brian. A couple of years ago, I didn't even know his name – to my shame. He was just one of those chaps in blue overalls you saw about the School, and you said 'Good morning' and that was that. Now, if I want anything done in my office to do with cleaning, repairing, or moving, I ask Brian and it is done. He is courteous, helpful, prompt, and reliable – invaluable. John fixes locks for me; Eddie restores old framed photographs. And so on.

I knew the Bursar's staff before, but I see them much more frequently now. My office is in the same wing, so sheer geography dictates that we meet more often. But I have to make enquiries about money from time to time, I have to ask for stationery, I have to go somewhere to find someone who can get me out of trouble when the photo-copier breaks down – so Rosalie or Pam come to the rescue.

Rosalie, incidentally, is a repository of endless information, gossip and legend about the School's past. One day I intend to put together a piece to incorporate some at least of her reminiscences. I even have a title for it: 'Picking Rosalie's Brains'. I have given her a list of questions which I should like her to answer. But she is a very busy lady; quite apart from her work in the Bursar's office, she is a piano teacher and a local magistrate. So it may be a long time before Rosalie has her brains properly picked.

And, if Rosalie is a repository of titbits and anecdote, Helen Clark is a veritable university library of it. My office is just above the Headmaster's and Secretaries' offices, and I often have to go past them to get to the machines for copying and cutting and so on. And I have discovered that if you ask Helen the answer to one question, you usually finish up with the answers to another twenty or thirty questions you didn't know you were going to ask.

I have discovered that being an archivist makes people talk to you. 'Have you come across so-and-so? He must have been here – oh – about fifty or sixty years ago, I suppose.' It may be that they only want to know 'just where is your office?' It may be that they have an odd idea of what you do – 'is that where you have your little cubby-hole?' But, whatever it is, people talk to you.

It makes people show you things. 'I've got these maps; they've been in my lab. for years. Any use to you?' Well, they may be; they may not. But you have made yet another contact.

It makes people write to you too. Old blazers have been sent in, old caps, old athletics cups, old Fortescue Medals. Letters of enquiry – 'my grandfather used to work as a School servant; my grandmother and mother used to be seamstresses'. Could I find out anything about them? More contact. And you get some nice grateful letters back.

If you take the trouble to put something from the Archive on a notice board, someone will talk to you about it. Especially if it is an old photograph. People cannot resist an old photograph. There must be something about sepia. I would suggest it as a helpful colour to hypnotists.

You find yourself making contacts outside the School. And I don't mean just old boys and girls. When the Archive was set up, the local press gave us a little write-up. At intervals since, at the instigation of the the the staff's press officer, Judith Whittal-Williams, I have provided bulletins about this and that, for consumption by the local media, and this has led to photographs being taken and journalists coming down from a local TV station. 'Just turn a little this way, Mr Coates. And hold the document up – look at it – a bit higher – that's lovely.' 'We'll just take another from the corner – I want to get a shot of that gorgeous minute book on your desk. If you'd just have it open – there. Terrific.' 'Now – I'll ask you a question, and when you reply, I want you to look just to the left of the camera.' 'Don't worry, Mr Coates, we can do it again. Most people get it wrong first time.' (Aren't they kind!)

So – do I look forward to being a media celebrity? Well, hardly. But it has all proved unexpected, interesting, and fun. What are the plans? Lots. There is no end of organising to do for a start. Storage is a problem. I have the office the Headmaster talked about, and it is new, clean, private and secluded. (And – don't tell anybody – it has one of the finest views in the whole School.) But we are short on shelves, cupboards and cabinets. Much of what we have is stored in those cardboard boxes that file paper is delivered in. I have to devise, for instance, a scheme for preserving a whole honeycomb of rolled-up school photographs. Those minute-books I spoke of are, many of them, in poor condition, and could do with re-binding. Ideally, I could do with large albums in which to store and preserve dozens of very large (and remarkably well-preserved) team photographs – football, cricket, rugby, shooting, athletics (they seem to have very long, thin calves and ankles in athletics teams). All those serious faces and folded arms. In the old ones, all those enormous football boots.

Ideally, everything needs to be comprehensively labelled, catalogued and cross-referenced. One over-the-rainbow dream is to have, in the end, a separate file on every pupil who has ever been through the School. Since 1858. These days, it is now commonplace to talk of data bases and instant retrieval and so on, and these systems obviously have their place. But, in an archive, there is no substitute for a physical file, containing the original documents, which you can actually get hold of. You may one day be able to look up a governor's letter or a pupil's report from 1882 on a computer, but there is nothing like having the actual piece of paper in your hand.

It would be nice to publish something about the Archive and about the School. If you are reading this, it will mean that we have gone some way towards achieving that particular ambition. There ought to be ways of involving the pupils in the Archive, depending upon the availability of time and space. So far we have managed one or two sixth-form projects based on Archive material, and one or two actual lessons with juniors. This sphere can be developed. Attempts have been made to publicise the Archive among the old members of the School – a small stand at Old Boys' Day, a mention in despatches in Speech Day reports and O.W.B.A. after-dinner speeches. We have sold several copies of R.F. Delderfield's collection of stories about the School, *Tales Out of School* – and there are plenty more on offer. We have printed, and sold, Archive Christmas cards; there are more possibilities there. If you tap into the West Buckland website on the Internet, you will find a section devoted to the Archive – and very 'gothic' it is too! Other interviews with the media might lead to something else – who knows?

Just as Alice did not know what she was going to find when she fell down the hole, so we do not know what the future will hold for the Archive. But, as with Alice in Wonderland, the doors are opening all the time. And, as with Alice again, it all promises to get curiouser and curiouser.

THE BOOK AND THE GENESIS

Our parish magazine, in the year 2000, is a paper-back job, of about twenty pages or so, run up by a hard-working, well-meaning lady in the next parish. If it were not for the editing and copying facilities offered by word-processors, I doubt if we would have even that – and that is no disrespect to the lady editor, because she is a busy person.

In 1857, the year before the School was founded, the village of West Buckland also had a book devoted to it. It contained 170 pages, it was properly bound, with hard covers, and it was professionally printed, by 'T. Brettell, Rupert Street, Haymarket'. It had gold lettering on the front and the spine – *West Buckland Year Book*. After 143 years, it is still in surprisingly good nick.

I have no idea for how many years this annual volume was printed, but whatever its print run, it is a remarkable testimony to the public spirit and hard work of whatever group of people who were responsible for it. Quite apart from the literary and editorial work involved, imagine the time-consuming effort required, in a tiny village several miles from the nearest town, before electricity, telephones and railways, never mind motorways and computers.

One suspects they sprang from the middle class; the aristocracy and the gentry would have looked down on it as a most un-gentlemanly thing to do (the whole point of being a gentleman was that one did not 'work'), and the 'labouring classes' (as everyone else was prone to label them) were too damned busy, too damned poor, and too damned tired (and illiterate) to think of doing it. Young men like David Livingstone, who, after a twelve-hour shift in the mills, were prepared to sit down by a guttering candle and study medicine into the night, were extremely rare.

It is easy to condemn the Victorian middle classes. They are portrayed all too often as smug, self-righteous, overfed, narrow-minded Pharisaic hypocrites who knew what was best for everybody. Each of these adjectival accusations carries in it some measure of truth, but, even taken together, they do not amount to the whole truth.

These good souls believed in the value of knowledge, almost for its own sake. Many of the pieces in the *Year Book* read like pages from the *Encyclopaedia Britannica*. The article on 'Fishing in Devon', for instance, is chock full of detail about where to fish, how to fish, types of fly, Devon rivers, with a paean of praise for Devon scenery thrown in for good measure. The section on 'Devonshire Cream' is bursting with esoteric lore about gauze strainers and scalding and

skimming and charcoal fires. It goes on to regale the hungry reader with many examples of similar recipes being prepared in Naples and Athens and Constantinople – even the Crimea and India. (Remember this was 1857, and the battles of the Crimean War were still fresh in people's minds.) This was followed by speculations on the history of Devonshire Cream, which embraced references to the Crimea (again), the Celts, 'a Trojan chief named Brutus', theories about the origins of the name 'Devon', St Michael's Mount, Druids, and King Arthur and the Round Table. It ended with the claim that doctors were now recommending it for 'consumptive patients, instead of the far less palatable Cod's Liver Oil'.

They believed particularly in the value of new knowledge. The pages of the *Year Book* carry articles teeming with information on the latest machines, the best practice in stock-breeding, pig-raising, poultry-keeping and so on. One contributor made a good case for introducing decimal weights, measures and coinage. In 1857.

They were interested in the world outside Devon. The Year Book contained a piece about a riding tour of Cornwall, and another about pig-hunting in New Zealand. There was a poem about emigrants, and another on Frederick the Great. And a quite inexplicable inclusion about 'Gertrude of Wyoming'.

They were proud of their country – witness the constant references to the recent Crimean War, and the sacrifices of the brave soldiers in that distant land (how many of them could have unerringly pointed to it on the map?) There was a poem printed near the end, dedicated 'to the Guards returning from the Crimea'.

They were proud of their village – they took delight in recording 'some of the successful steps in improvement taken by "Our Parish" in the last few years'. There followed detailed extracts from the *North Devon Journal* about the 'first agricultural show at West Buckland, 18 September 1854', the 'second agricultural show, 3 October 1855', and the initial meetings of the United Parishes' Farming Society.

Earl Fortescue agreed to be President of the new society, and the Revd J.L. Brereton, rector of West Buckland, said he would be the secretary. The first meeting took place at the Earl's seat at Castle Hill. In view of the later commitment of these two gentlemen to the cause of the West Buckland Farm and County School, do we pause in wonder at the variety and extent of their activities (there may well have been others, which could have been recorded in the pages of other year books), or was it simply that, as the resident aristocrat and cleric respectively, it was inevitable that they would have been asked to be the president and secretary of nearly everything? At the second meeting of the United Parishes' Farming Society, in 1856, Brereton was presented with a silver inkstand, and Fortescue, in his speech, referred to a gold pencil case presented to Brereton by his parish school, and a silver cream jug given to him by the parish clothing club.

For all I know, Brereton was also the editor of the *Year Book* itself.

He would have certainly shared the views of other middle-class worthies who also believed strongly in trying to unite the village. They may have gone about it in a somewhat heavy-handed way, but they meant well, and they believed what they said.

It disturbed them, for instance, that the 'labouring class' did not play more games, did not have more respectable ways of passing the time when they were not working. They were disturbed, in short, by the fondness of the 'labouring class' for the public house and everything that went with it – drunkenness, rowdiness, and public damage. The cynic may claim that they were concerned only for their own peace of mind and for the safety of their property, but I think this is unfair. They were no more afraid of a bunch of village lads stomping round the village on a Saturday night than a suburban resident today is of a gang of joy-riders or a crowd of defeated football supporters.

While they did deplore this anti-social activity as most undesirable and most un-Christian, they did also try to do something about it beside simply complain and moralise. They discussed the ways of providing 'reasonable occupation and amusement for the labouring classes in leisure hours' – by means of things like 'libraries, clubs, lectures and institutes'. They extolled the value of a 'public green' in every town and village. And this was not merely pipe-dreaming; they offered the very practical calculation that 'a very small subscription would generally supply enough to pay the rent of several acres, which would readily be given at moderate terms by the landlords for the use of all those who would be members of the club'. So they were prepared to put their money on the table as well as their foot on the soapbox.

Cricket, they believed, would not only be healthy; it would draw young men away from the public bar, and above all it would unite all classes in the comradeship of the team. It is interesting to see that this idea of the value of the team was not primarily an educational one, although the public schools were quick to catch on to it. It seems to have been a sincere attempt by the class in the middle – between gentleman and worker – to create, at any rate in one small part of the week, an atmosphere in which all could share, if not as equals, then at least as team-members and fellow-performers.

The nineteenth century was a time which saw an explosion of population, especially among the 'labouring classes'. Coincident with this was a gradual relaxation of the penal code, as more and more crimes were released from the death penalty. The propertied, 'respectable', 'responsible' members of society were anxious to keep this growing mass under control. The honest ones realised that the rope was no longer going to do it. Neither was prison. Neither was hectoring or lecturing, or the police force; there were too many of them.

There were only two ways left – to replace fear of the rope with fear of Divine punishment; or to try and give them something 'worthwhile' to do. Hence the inclusion of fifty pages of printed sermons at the back of the book, with the very practical thought that, even if working families could not read, there were enough children from the growing village school who could, and who could therefore read them out loud to their families on the Sabbath. Hence the exhortations about cricket and 'foot-ball' and the helpful printing of the rules of the two games. ('Each side tries to kick the ball beyond the line opposite to it, and the side which gets the greater number of games in this way, is the winner. The ball may be stopped, but must not be taken up in the hands.')

It was well meant, but it approached the problem from the standpoint of their own experience of life, instead of from the standpoint of the 'labouring classes' ' experience of life. They did not have the knowledge, or the imagination, or the resources, to try and go deeper and remove some of the causes of their poverty and overwork and sullen violence and recourse to drink. They tried to go into competition with drink instead of trying to kill the need to drink.

Nevertheless, to their credit, they did not leave the 'labouring class' to rot; they did try. And for all we know, their well-meaning earnestness, which to this more sophisticated generation looks naive and prim and auntie-ish, may have struck more of a chord than we give them credit for. We cannot know what the 'labouring class' thought of them, because none of them wrote it down. We do know, though, that parents and pupils at Brereton's village school gave him a gold pencil case. Gold. And they were not well off.

This is not an exhaustive survey of life in West Buckland village in 1857, and it is not a complete account of the Revd Brereton's activities. But I think it is a safe deduction to make that Brereton was a fair example of the mid-Victorian do-gooder – in the nicest possible way. Over-respectable for our taste he may seem now – even slightly prissy. But he was conscientious, he was industrious, he was constantly thinking of new ideas, he believed in his village and in the people who made up his flock. And his flock, some of them at any rate, were grateful for his efforts.

It was beyond him to think of secondary teaching for the 'labouring class', when he had barely got the village primary school going. Perhaps he felt that he had made his gesture towards lower-class education, and that it was time to turn his attention elsewhere. But he was clearly aware of the great liberating influence of education in general. Looking back, at that very primary school, and at the parish clothing club, and at the 'United Parishes' Farming Society', and the desire for a cricket green; and given Earl Fortescue's known interest in education – it seems it was only going to be a matter of time before Brereton said one day to Fortescue, 'Look, sir, I've got this idea – about a secondary school, a different type of secondary school. . . '

The first home of the new school, from late 1858 to early 1859 – Miller's Farmhouse, Stoodleigh. There are Millers in the School to this day. This was the school which, in the words of the *Illustrated London News*, 'was started in an unpretending manner' – with just three pupils, all from Bishop's Tawton.

THE FORTESCUE FAMILY

Without this family of benefactors, the School would never have been founded and would never have survived.

The fourth Earl Fortescue (Governor 1905-32), who laid the Foundation Stone for the Memorial Hall.

Hugh, second Earl Fortescue, who laid the first Foundation Stone in 1860.

The fifth Earl Fortescue (Governor 1932-58), and his wife, also a Governor, died within a week of each other.

Lady Margaret Fortescue (Governor 1958-96), daughter of the fifth Earl Fortescue.

Lady Arran, Lady Margaret's daughter (a present Governor), continues the tradition into the sixth generation.

A Mature Student

On 24 May, 1859, the second Earl Fortescue attended the opening of the new dormitory of the Devon Farm and County School. After his speech, in which he praised the progress of the pioneer School, he presented a prize to a young farmer of twenty-five who had taken a year out, away from his farm, in order to study at the School. His lordship gave 'many strong expressions of his respect' to this worthy pupil, and reminded his audience that the Headmaster had 'specially alluded' to this pupil's 'uniform good conduct since entering the School'.

The Headmaster in question, Mr. J.H. Thompson, had been appointed the previous year, at the age of twenty-one.

[There cannot be many schools, then or now, who can claim a prize presentation at which the winner was three years older than the Headmaster.]

❖ HIGH HOPES ❖

On Tuesday, 24 May 1859, Queen Victoria celebrated her fortieth birthday. So, too, did many of her subjects. The occasion was marked, in the village of West Buckland, North Devon, by a public lunch. It was, we are told, 'a very tasteful and abundant lunch', and it was provided by Mrs Tamlyn, the wife of the farmer on whose farm the lunch was being served. It was attended by a hundred and fifty local worthies. Which says a lot for Mrs Tamlyn's energy and stamina as well as for her culinary skill.

Mrs Tamlyn was also the Matron of the new educational establishment which had moved to the farm the previous January. It had been set up barely six months before – in November 1858, to be precise, at another nearby farm, Stoodleigh. But the original school roll of three had risen to eleven (ten boarders and one day boy), and there was no longer enough room. Hence the move. By Easter, the number had gone up to seventeen, and there was not enough room at the second farm, Tideport, either.

So a new dormitory was built, to accommodate twenty boys. (Shortly afterwards, two more buildings were added – one for lessons, and one for meals.) All were made of wood. It was in order to celebrate the opening of this new dormitory – as well as the Queen's birthday – that the hundred and fifty 'ladies and gentlemen' assembled – inside it.

It was a distinguished gathering for an Exmoor village. Fourteen clergymen, for a start – the incumbents of surrounding villages – as well as the Revd J.L. Brereton, the vicar of West Buckland itself. So it could hardly have been more respectable. Most were accompanied by their wives, which made it even more respectable. Wives seemed to be much more 'there' in those days; is this a partial explanation for the greater stability of marriages in Victorian times? Or is it a symptom of the stability rather than a cause?

The Mayor of Barnstaple was present, and his wife too. An ample cross-section of local farmers and businessmen, and 'many others'. Naturally, a fair number of relatives and friends of pupils attended, most of them, we are told, with charming reticence, 'accompanied by ladies and friends'. That's right – 'friends' of 'friends'.

And if that is not impressive enough, the most eminent member of the gathering, by far, was the Earl Fortescue – with, inevitably, his wife, accompanied by another 'lady', Miss Geale.

No meeting in those days was complete without a hefty dose of speeches, and the company certainly got its money's worth that day. One from Brereton, one

from the Headmaster of the fledgling school, J.H. Thompson, and one from Earl Fortescue. A fourth came from one of the attendant clergymen, the Revd H.S. Pinder, of Bratton Fleming, who had been one of the examiners of the School's pupils at the recent Easter examinations. He 'begged leave' to 'testify to the extreme accuracy with which the pupils had been instructed', and he offered his 'most cordial congratulations on the prosperous state of the School'.

Nor was that the end of the proceedings; the village choir sang 'several glees', and 'the pupils of the School were put through their drill and sword exercise by their instructor, Serjeant [sic] Hill'. (Sword exercise!) Then – still not finished – there were 'various outdoor amusements', concluding with 'tea and music' (more work for the indefatigable Mrs Tamlyn, assuming she had finished the washing up from lunch).

When one reads of nineteenth-century public entertainments, one is often struck by the stamina of the audience (never mind Mrs Tamlyn's). Subscription concerts would have interminable programmes of concertos and symphonies. Theatrical productions would often have a one-acter as a prologue or epilogue to the main three-acter at the top of the bill. And so with dinners and lunches – soups and entrées and main dishes and desserts, to say nothing of toasts and songs and recitations. At the Devon County School Old Boys' Dinner in 1907, there were eight courses, and a total of twenty-three toasts and replies and songs and recitations. Look at the programme that Toad sketched out for his homecoming dinner in *The Wind in the Willows*. No wonder the Rat and the Badger said he couldn't do it.

So, why? Was it greater greed, greater affluence, greater appetite for culture? Or was it that, public transport – indeed any transport – being what it was, people simply didn't get out very much; so, when they did, they made a meal of it – to coin a phrase.

After this particular meal, Lady Fortescue, who was presiding, introduced the Revd J.L. Brereton to the gathering. Observe that it was she who was presiding, not her husband, though he was also there. So the printed record, with commendable attention to protocol, noted that she was 'accompanied by Earl Fortescue'. The Earl was not 'accompanied' by her ladyship.

After the necessary, and willing, drinking of the loyal toast to many royal happy returns, Brereton got down to business. He hoped that the new wooden building in which they were now gathered would long be preserved as 'a memorial to the infancy of the

School'. So he was looking a long way ahead. He thanked Lord Fortescue for his moral and financial support. He sang the praises of the new Headmaster, Mr J.H. Thompson, and asserted that he (Thompson) was already discharging his new duties 'to the manifest improvement of the pupils, and the great satisfaction of their parents'.

He admitted that 'the agricultural feature of the plan' was experiencing 'some practical difficulties', but that that feature 'would be perseveringly developed'. This may require a little explanation. Brereton and Thompson's original concept was of a twofold school. One would provide that solid education for the middle classes that was the biggest bee in Brereton's bonnet. This was the 'Devon County School' bit. The second envisaged a school of practical farming, where the pupils would work on an actual farm that was part of the School, the profits of which would go to defray the pupils' fees. The Utopian dimension of this idea seems to have been a school which would become entirely self-supporting. Remember, the School was originally known, and advertised, as the 'West Buckland Farm and County School'.

Having played, as it were, his losing trick, and got it out of the way, Brereton moved to his stronger suits – the development of an Upper and a Preparatory section to the County School, and the new dormitory itself, the twenty beds of which 'would be very shortly filled'. (And they were.)

Here he came to what P.G. Wodehouse would call the 'nub'. This was the future development of the School, which meant more pupils, which meant more facilities, which meant the provision of permanent accommodation, which meant a move, which meant. . . well, which meant more money.

It is always a thankless task to get people to part with money. It is hard enough to back them individually into a corner and get them to cough up, but to do it in public, *en masse*, out in the open, up on the platform, is infinitely harder, and demands a silver tongue, an iron determination, and a brass neck, plus the wit to jump at a golden opportunity when you see one. And a hundred and fifty assorted ladies and gentlemen of North Devon, under one roof, loaded to the gunwales with Mrs Tamlyn's pies and pasties, admiring the twenty new beds on the new floor of the new dormitory of the new School – this was just such an opportunity.

Brereton seems, like so many Victorian reformers, to have been a curious mixture – busy cleric, family man, idealist, indefatigable writer of pamphlets and arranger of public meetings and subscription lists – almost a parody of the energetic changer of the world who is a source of pride and weariness to his family and supporters at one and the same time. Yet he did not enjoy good health, and he lived in an obscure Devon village well off the beaten track between main towns.

It is true, too, that other schemes he hatched had a trick of fizzling out. Jon Edmunds, in his history of West Buckland School, refers to other projects, in Cambridge and Norfolk, which, ultimately, came to nothing. It speaks volumes for his imagination, resilience, and drive that he was willing to try again.

And look at what he was up against. For a start, he was up against his own Church. In the days when more ink was spilt on the place of denominational religion in education than on almost anything else – more even than on the bombshell of Darwinism – Brereton championed an open approach. A boy was to have a Christian education, naturally, but not a rigid Anglican or Anglo-Catholic or Methodist one. This sentiment would certainly not attract many Anglican or Anglo-Catholic or Methodist parents, one would suppose, and how many were left? If anybody was in any further doubt, Brereton made it clear that the new Headmaster was not going to be a clergyman at all. (Thompson did later take holy orders, but almost certainly for reasons not directly connected with the founder's ideas.)

Nor was he going to be a graduate; the world was to understand that this School was not going to be just another country crammer in Classics for the sons of gentlemen.

So he was up against the Established Church, and a lot of Nonformity as well. He was up against the lofty disdain of the monied classes, if indeed they took any notice of him at all, except to sneer at yet another busybody in a dog-collar. And, perhaps most daunting of all, he was up against Devon farmers and tradesmen, who can be harder to move than a dry dock full of battleships.

There survives in the Archive no actual written record of their views, partly, one suspects, because such gentlemen were notoriously unwilling to commit themselves even verbally, never mind on paper. But, if you cock your head and listen to the rustles in the reeds of time, you might hear such a man holding forth in the saloon bar of the *George* on market day – 'that there Berton an' 'is school. I daun' know. If you want to turn a pound, you turn a furrow; you daun' turn a page in some book. An' 'oo waunts a son wot spouts longer wurds than what 'ee do hiszelf?'

Other, more educated, critics also impugned Brereton's ideas and motives in the corrrespondence columns of the local paper, one going so far as to liken the new school to a union workhouse.

Brereton rose to the occasion, riding on the back of a truly magnificent charger of supreme confidence. It was the doctor-musician-philosopher Albert Scheitzer who observed that the first pre-requisite of any worthwhile venture, for it to have the slightest chance of success, was confidence. Brereton must have possessed that, and in abundance.

Secondly, he had the shrewdness to see past his own idealism. Perhaps he had learned from his previous failures. Certainly he realised that letters and subscription lists and public meetings were not enough. For his scheme to succeed, he needed a big name, he needed publicity, and he needed clout. If he got the first, the other two would follow. Hugh, the second Earl Fortescue, of Castle Hill in Filleigh, brought all three in full measure. He was landed aristocracy, he was established, he was Lord Lieutenant of the county, he was interested in education, and he lived up the road. Tailor-made. And even his lordship had had his doubts, as he very honestly confessed in his speech after Brereton's. But, as he surveyed the new building, he said he wished to make up for his temporary weakening of resolve by paying for it. You couldn't have it fairer than that. (The Fortescues were to remain the financial mainstay of the School for generations to come.)

Thirdly, he made, it seems, a sensible choice of Headmaster. Joseph Thompson was neither a graduate nor a cleric, so would not offend religious sensibilities or excite bourgeois suspicions about patrician attitudes being foisted on their sons by the back door, as it were. The very fact that Thompson was an unknown quantity may have told in his favour. Certainly his youth should have done. He was only twenty-one – too young to have absorbed the prejudices of a superior class.

Finally, Brereton showed diplomacy of a high order when it came to discussing with his audience of farmers and tradesmen the matters of the future, and, above all, of money. Like General Booth of the Salvation Army, he did not see why the Devil should have a monopoly of the best tunes, or, in his case, the best techniques. He set about borrowing from the Great Sin Salesman the can of oil in which resides flattery and reassurance.

It was not for him, he said, to lay down the law about the form the future school should take. The School was only in the experimental stage. And he certainly did not expect his audience to contribute to a mere experiment. Dear me, no. But, when he and Mr Thompson had shown that their new School was modern, holy, and would enhance their sons' chances in life, why – then he had every confidence that farmers and tradesmen would join the landlords and gentry in a cause which they could see was so clearly and so much their own. In short, like the best wide boys who make you an offer you can't refuse, he was giving his audience a splendid chance to do them selves a spot of good.

Brereton was certainly rare among reformers in that not only was he prepared to commit his time, his efforts, and his reputation to his ideas; he was prepared to commit his money – and his children. He put funds into the early School, and he sent his son there too. This was a far cry from those Labour politicians who trumpeted the virtues of the comprehensive system of education, while quietly sending their children off to expensive public schools. Interestingly, too, one of his daughters later married Thompson.

When Earl Fortescue rose to speak, he congratulated Brereton, and he congratulated Thompson, and he expressed the hope that the School would one day be numbered 'not merely by tens but by hundreds' – which showed a striking blend of unfounded optimism and uncanny prescience.

When his lordship sat down, and the farmers and tradesmen and vicars, and their wives and 'friends', applauded, were they simply carried away by fruit cup and sherry trifle? Or were too many of them his lordship's tenants, who knew what was good for them?

Or was it that they were genuinely convinced of the validity of Brereton's ideas? Many of those present could not have had much of an education themselves, apart from the clergymen. Many of them perhaps would not have agreed with the taproom philosopher in the *George*, and honestly wanted to provide a better chance in life for their sons.

From that royal birthday meeting and bunfight in a wooden shed, among twenty new beds, the School grew from 17 in 1859 to 150 by the mid-1870s, and, with a lot of ups and downs, to nearly 600 in the year 2000. A long way. When you look back at them, as through the wrong end of the telescope of hindsight, they look very small indeed.

What was it like, to have been there? What did they really think? Amid the cold beef and the Devonshire cream, the gaiters and waistcoats, the bonnets and crinolines, the drainpipe trousers and the stovepipe hats, the hair nets and the mutton-chop whiskers, the calloused hands and the blue veins in the noses, the rustic residue on the soles of the boots and the cheap perfume from Barnstaple chemists – amid all that, what was really going on? What was their vision?

What would they think if they could see the place now? As Sam Goldwyn once said, 'If they were alive today, they would turn in their graves.'

An early print of the permanent School buildings. This is a rare three-quarter view which illustrates more of the part behind the front façade on the left.

An article from the *Illustrated London News* of 9 November, 1861, recording the genesis, building, and opening of the 'Devon County School' on 8 October. It is well worth a read. Note the estimated cost – £2000.

The Foundation Stone laid by the second Earl Fortescue, who sadly died just days before the opening of the building almost exactly a year later. Even now, 140 years on, while not everyone might subscribe wholeheartedly to the religious sentiments here expressed, it is difficult to disagree with the aspirations – 'the extension of sound and practical education'.

THE FOUNDATION STONE
OF THIS SCHOOL WAS LAID BY
EARL FORTESCUE K.G.
OCTᴿ 4ᵀᴴ 1860.

"In humble hope that the Great Architect of the Universe the Maker of Heaven and earth the Giver of all Good, will bless and prosper the work this day commenced, and that the School to be raised will prove, under the Divine blessing, an institution for the promotion of God's glory in the extension of sound and practical education, in the diffusion of useful knowledge, upon the imperishable foundation of Divine truth."

THE
Devon County School Register.

No. I.   JULY, 1863.

THE object of this unpretending little publication is to give some information regarding the School and its progress, which may be interesting to its friends.

Though this Periodical is intended more particularly to record what may be of interest to present and past pupils, to their parents and friends, and to those who have taken an immediate and personal interest in the school, yet it may possibly be of interest also to the increasing class who are beginning to take part in movements for the establishment of County Schools in different parts of the country.

It will probably be continued half-yearly, or perhaps even quarterly.

The very first page of the very first *Register*, July, 1863. The last number appeared in 1997. Its name survives – just – in the title of the new magazine: *The Three R's*, which stand for 'Read', 'Reap', and 'Register'.

⬛ DATING IT ⬛

There is something about a yellowing sheet of old newspaper. Whether you dig it out of an archive, find it in the bottom of a newly-purchased antique chest of drawers, or simply come across it in the loft when you are obsessed with searching for something else, at once there is the compulsion to stop and have a look at it.

You at once credit it with special qualities which, if it were articulate and honest, it would never claim to possess. Unless of course it bore a headline like 'WAR DECLARED' or 'NAPOLEON DIES' or 'ENGLAND WIN A TEST MATCH' or something like that. No. Most old newspaper sheets in the bottoms of drawers are from some middle page of mind-numbing ordinariness in a provincial journal of impenetrable obscurity. Yet it is anything but ordinary to the reader who finds it a hundred years later.

Just as other people's books, CDs and washing up are more interesting than your own, so the dullest titbits of news from another century take on a quality of readability that is quite irresistible.

More.

If it happens that the cutting or the column has obviously been taken out because of an item of peculiar interest to a person or to an institution, then the reader, if he is connected with that person or institution, is naturally intrigued.

So, when, as the Archivist of West Buckland School, I come across an article from the *Exeter Gazette* headed 'MIDDLE CLASS EDUCATION – Devon County School', I want to read it. Indeed I need to read it. ('Devon County School' was the School's original name.)

Especially as the article informs me that the meeting it was recording was 'one of the most important which has taken place at the School since the opening of the institution'.

Certificates and prizes were handed out to pupils successful in the School and in the Oxford Local Examinations. So it was Speech Day. But it was more than that; it was a meeting of shareholders too. The Chairman, the Revd J.L. Brereton (the School's founder), naturally gave his 'state of the union' message to the assembled well-wishers. You know the sort of thing you hear at modern speech days – the School was doing very well indeed and the under-twelve ping-pong team had won all its matches with record scores. In this case, the Revd Brereton was pleased to report that the School was now 'fairly entitled to call itself a self-supporting institution'; that the number of boarders had risen from 62 to 82; that 12 day boys were now attending; and that he and his fellow-directors had pleasure and confidence in submitting their report. (Lots of 'hear hear's'.)

Better was to come. The Revd Brereton felt so sure of the School's future that he proposed to ask for powers to approach the general public to take up the additional capital required to pay off the mortgage and other debts to the National Provincial Bank and to 'go on in a state of increasing prosperity in future years'. ('Hear hear.')

Just to get the ball rolling, the Earl Fortescue rose to announce that he had heard from a well-wisher and 'constant friend' of the School, a Mr Sillifant, who wished his name to be put down for £50. He hoped, naturally, that where Mr Sillifant led, many others would follow. ('Hear hear.')

After sundry other business, the company adjourned to the 'large school-room' and 'partook of an elegant luncheon (provided by Mr Stone, of the "Fortescue Arms Hotel", Barnstaple)'. It was a pretty distinguished company too – Earl of Devon, Lord Fortescue, the Earl of Harrowby, Lord and Lady Taunton, a mayor of South Molton, and an M.P., a Knight of the Garter, a Companion of the Order of the Bath, a knighthood, and no fewer than twelve clerical collars. Look at the previous chapter again. You have to hand it to West Buckland when it comes to whipping in the celebrities.

So much for the relevant side, the West Buckland side. But turn the cutting over to the other side, and at once you are plunged into a new world of enthralling happenings. Within minutes you become acquainted with the workings of the Italian Parliament, the Federal Council of Switzerland, the Central Committee of all the Schleswig-Holstein Political Associations, and the opening of the Transylvanian diet (as it's Transylvania, I bet there's plenty of blood on the menu – ho!ho!)

How many provincial newspapers today carry news items, in detail, of events in eighteen different countries? And even if they did, how many modern readers, despite their modern sophisticated education, care much about what happens in Austria, Croatia, Poland, Turkey, Algeria, or Jamaica? Well, they did then. They would have been suitably shocked to learn that, in the 'Negro Rising in Jamaica', 'the barbarities committed could only be paralleled by the account of the Indian mutiny; the women were more barbarous than the men'. They would have nodded sagely when they read that 'Austria has resolved to reduce her army in Venetia'. And they would no doubt have reached for their pens to dash off a letter of disgust to the editor when they saw that, in India, 'an English girl has been sold by her parents to the Chief of Chutna for 3000 rupees'.

If foreign news of another century makes compelling reading, the adverts of another century become positively addictive. What about 'Another Cure of Asthma by Dr Locock's Pulmonic Wafers'? Indispensable for 'asthma [naturally], consumption, coughs, and all disorders of the breath and lungs'. Oh – and they also 'have a pleasant taste'. Or 'Mrs S.A. Allen's Hair Restorer and Zylobalsamum'? They 'act upon the hair as does the dew upon the flowers'. Available from the pharmacies of Mr J.M. Rendall, of Exeter, Plymouth, and Torquay.

But one must tear oneself away. The document has to be properly read, assessed for its historical value, and, most important, dated. Just when did the Revd J.L. Brereton make his proud report to the assembled shareholders, and ask the generous public to subscribe further capital to the worthy cause of Devon County School's mortgage?

As luck would have it, the half of the page that had been cut away was the half that contained the newspaper's date. As luck would further have it, neither the Revd Brereton nor the Earl Fortescue made any convenient reference to a county cricket match or a general election that could be precisely pinpointed by recourse to the relevant encyclopaedias.

But of course – 'Eureka, Watson!' Turn over, and there were hosts of references to contemporary events which would solve the problem at once. Well, not quite. I am not sufficiently acquainted with the internal history of Turkey to be able to deduce a date from the intelligence that 'the expedition against the insurgents of Kosan Dagh had suffered a reverse'. Nor is it much use to me to be told that 'the National Croatian party have resolved to propose a union of Croatia, Hungary, and Sclavonia'. My grasp of Sclavonian politics is not what it used to be.

By the same token, I am not expert on the policies of censorship pursued by the Prussian Government, the treatment of political prisoners in Galicia, or the incidence of cholera on the banks of the Ganges.

Admittedly, I got close with a reference by Fortescue to the recent death of an 'illustrious statesman', but that only narrowed the chances; it didn't eliminate them. Closer still by a mention, in the American news, of President Johnson, who was in office from 1865 to 1868 – and was the first president to be impeached. (He got off by one vote.)

I was then reminded of an elementary lesson that ought to be learned, and is often forgotten, by historians – read ALL the document.

I turned the cutting over again to the second side, and read down to the bottom, right down to the bottom – beyond the Negro Rising in Jamaica, beyond Dr Locock's cure for asthma, beyond the very bottom line. And there, underneath everything, was the answer: 'Exeter: Printed and published by and for CHARLES WESCOMB, of the Vineyard, Castle Street, in the Precinct of Bradninch, in the City of Exeter, at his Printing Office, No. 236, High Street, in the Parish of St Stephen, in the City aforesaid, – Friday, Nov. 24, 1865.'

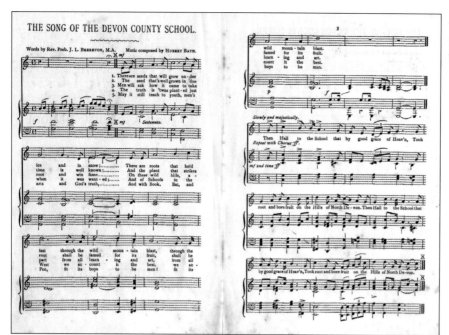

The School Song, words by the indefatigable Revd J.L. Brereton. When was it last sung?

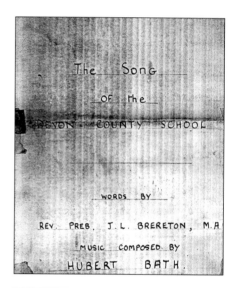

A manuscript version of the School Song, but though the paper is old, the handwriting somehow does not look nineteenth Century. So it is unlikely to be original.

Some public occasions in West Buckland's early history would see up to a dozen newspaper reporters on the premises, and, according to J.H. Thompson, the first Head, 'special arrangements would be made at Barnstaple post office to send reports of particular speeches to the London press'.

Where the Buck Stops

The Lillywhite's *Cricketers' Companion* for 1870 reviewed, among many others of course, the Devon County School cricket team of 1869. This was proudly reprinted in the *Register*. Included in the remarks on the form and skill of the various players was this rare tribute to the humblest and most unsung hero in any cricket team: W.F.E. Read was described as an 'excellent long stop, the best ever at the School'.

[Is there an Old Boy since on whose behalf anyone wishes to challenge that claim? Or who wishes to challenge it himself?]

The prizes for one of the very early speech days at the School, in 1863, were presented by the Archbishop of Canterbury. One of these prize books has been presented to the Archive.

On 26 August 1869, West Buckland School (admittedly including some masters) played a cricket match against 'Northmolton', on the School ground, and won by 278 runs. [Which must have taken some doing.]

❀ A Very Happy Day ❀

The pages of the early *Registers* are full of lists of prizewinners and successes in examinations. And why not? The young School wanted to parade its triumphs, to flex its academic muscles in the ring so long dominated by the public school heavyweights with fashionable connections and extensive endowments. This, after all, was a 'middle-class' school, and the middle classes in the nineteenth century were determined to prove themselves in every field of activity. They wanted to rival the aristocracy in business, industry, commerce, and, inevitably, politics. Quite naturally therefore they wanted their schools to be considered as effective in their way as the older, 'established' institutions like the Eton's and the Harrow's.

Later on in the nineteenth century, these county schools began to change. Just as the middle classes themselves moved from attempting rivalry with the aristocracy to attempting emulation of it – for instance, in buying land and becoming the country gentleman, like the Knights on Exmoor, in accepting decorations and peerages – so their schools, having been set up as deliberately different from the public schools, slowly moved nearer to them, in tone, in curriculum, in aspiration. It can be no coincidence that Mr Thompson, having begun his service as Headmaster with neither degree nor dog collar, set about obtaining both before he finished. The 'Farm School' idea, much trumpeted at the outset, seems to have died pretty early. Latin crept into the timetable, albeit on a very selective basis. The time was to come when a headmaster was to be proud that he had become a member of the Headmasters' Conference – the great club of the public schools.

The full transition was to take a long time; indeed, a case can be made for the fact that it is not entirely complete even now. But in the very early days – say the first thirty years or so – there was a pioneering element in the School, a jaunty, bantam-weight bounce about it, a parochial pride in what it was doing, a sense of being 'on' to something different. I have not read other schools' magazines from the same period, so I cannot compare. But the early numbers of the *Register* are full of it. Its pages read like a proud parent drawing you from the doorstep into his parlour and showing you the family snaps. (There are those, of course, who would argue that this feature has by no means died out.)

In between the congratulations about academic successes and the times and winning distances in the Athletic Sports, and the interminable cricket scores, came intimate little jots of information like this:

'The services of W. Smith have been secured as professional bowler to the School Club during the month of August.' [The summer holidays ended in the last week of July.]

'During the last few days the School has been visited by the Head Masters of Winchester and Marlborough Colleges.' [Going up in the world.]

'A steam cooking apparatus has been erected in the school kitchen, under the superintendence of a London Engineering Firm.' [Note the awestruck capital letters.]

'Mr. Llewellyn, one of the masters, will be in Exeter on the Tuesday until the departure of the train from St David's Station at 4.08 p.m. for Barnstaple. His address will be the Railway Hotel, near St David's Station.' [Part of the arrangements for the start of the new term.]

'On Monday, 12 June [1871], three photographs were taken by Messrs. Britton; one of the school, with the boys in front; another of the Masters and Monitors; and another of the cricket eleven. They may be had of Mr Thomas, at the school, price three shillings each.' [Alas! We do not have them.]

In the *Register* of October, 1870, came this:

'Excursion. – During the Michaelmas Holidays, those boys who remained at the School made a Pic-nic Excursion to Lynton. The weather was very fine. Dinner was eaten under the shadow of the Castle Rock and a very happy day was spent.'

There it was, in between a reference to a couple of new prizes offered by ' "An Old Boy", who does not wish his name to be mentioned', and an account of the East Buckland Harvest Festival, the day of which had been 'ushered in by merry peals from the bells'.

By way of pardonable digression (I hope you will think it pardonable when you have read it), the latter entry also informed the attentive reader that, amongst other things: – 'the building had been decorated very tastefully, and reflected great credit on the masters and scholars of the Devon County School' [nothing your healthy Devon schoolboy loves more than a spot of church decoration in his free time]; 'the Revd Martin intoned the service' [not 'took' the service, or even 'conducted' it – 'intoned' it]; 'the Revd. W. Watson [acting Headmaster] and J. Bach [surely not Johann Sebastian?] read the lessons'; 'the sermon, preached by the Revd W. Burdett, vicar of Northmolton [sic], from Psalm lxviii., v. 10, which occupied about forty minutes in its delivery, was attentively listened to by an appreciative congregation' [that's what it says]; there was a 'substantial dinner after the service, in the County School dining-hall, where covers were laid for about 110, under the well-known admirable catering of Mr William Miller of West Buckland'; 'the usual loyal and patriotic toasts were given and rapturously received'; the after-dinner speeches were 'pithy and to the point, and promoted that good feeling which always ought to exist between employers and the employed'; and, finally, 'the collection after the service amounted to £3.17s. 4d.'

Five clergymen – for a harvest festival in 'this usually quiet little village' – not bad going. No, it was five; I didn't tell you about the Revd J.V. Roberts, who 'intoned the prayers after the anthem'.

However, to the matter under discussion – the 'Excursion' to Lynton. No great matter, to be sure. And the bare five lines present no immediate difficulties of comprehension. As P.G. Wodehouse would have said, anyone could have grabbed it straight off the bat. But have another look at it.

First, the language. People don't make 'excursions' nowadays; they go on 'trips'. Those who don't go are more likely to 'stay' than to 'remain'. Weather these days can be described as 'fine', but rarely 'very fine'. Now look at what they did when they got to the Valley of the Rocks. It says that they ate 'dinner'. Obviously it was some kind of midday meal, so one school of thought would argue that it should be 'lunch'. We are into a minefield here. Is it correct to call the midday meal 'lunch', or does that imply a patronising view of those who insist calling it 'dinner'? Why should you not call your main meal 'dinner' – especially if you take it at midday and don't eat a cooked meal in the evening? There is the further undeniable point that the midday meal in the schoolboy's day has, from time immemorial, been known as 'school dinner'.

Let us leave the minefield and examine the type of meal they had. They had a 'pic-nic'. (Interesting, the hyphen. If you look in early pages of the *Register* you will find 'foot-ball'). Why 'pic-nic'? Nothing to do with picking and choosing – 'Do you want the ham or the cheese, Hoskins? Come along, boy – make up your mind.' The dictionary will tell you that it comes from the French *'pique-nique'* – which is no great leap of the imagination, but a help. Just when you think you are on the trail, the dictionary tells you that the derivation is 'unknown'. A colleague who is herself French said that she had looked it up in a pretty thorough French etymological dictionary, which had offered the detail that the word *'pique-nique'* goes back as far as the seventeenth century. She also wondered whether the word had anything to do with the word *'piquer'*, which means 'to prick', and the word *'pique'*, which is an old word for a 'spike' or something similar. So – did they, in the seventeenth century, go for meals out of doors, and use their daggers to spear the morsels which took their eye on the tablecloth

spread over the grass? So perhaps it does mean 'pick and choose' in a roundabout sort of way after all. And, as a final *petit coup*, Martine told me that in many parts of France, it is still customary to say, not *'faire un pique-nique'*, but *'manger sur l'herbe'*.

Yes – well – let us move on.

Talking of derivations and meanings, how many members of the class can tell us when Michaelmas was? No, I thought so. It was 29 September actually, though I had to look it up myself to make sure. Why say 'Michaelmas' at all? Was it simply Victorian religiosity? Not entirely. The School year in those days was divided into four parts, not three – Lent or Easter, Summer, Michaelmas, and Christmas. With Easter, Midsummer, Michaelmas, and Christmas holidays in between. Jon Edmunds tells us in his *History of West Buckland School* that the three-term arrangement was introduced in 1878.

The Michaelmas break lasted barely a week, so it was quite likely that some pupils from distant parts could not easily get home and back again in the time. John Taylor Scott, for instance, is mentioned in the same number of the *Register*, and he hailed from North Shields. The Easter holiday was short too. So the chances are that many boys got home only twice a year – during midsummer and over Christmas. But with the spread of the railway system so rapidly across England, a journey home three times a year instead of only twice became more practicable – hence, as Jon Edmunds said, the three-term year.

Until 1878, then, it was a regular problem to cater for those pupils who could not get home for the short breaks at Easter and Michaelmas. The situation is similar to that of present pupils who live, say, in Thailand. Not many of them get home and back during the five-day holiday at the Whitsun half-term.

The Revd Watson, the Acting Headmaster while Mr Thompson was away at Cambridge for his degree studies, therefore arranged this excursion. How did he get them there? There was no railway. The Lynton to Barnstaple railway did not open till 1898. Obviously he couldn't make the poor devils walk. They didn't all own horses. So it must have been some kind of coach or cart. Think of it – all those miles from West Buckland to Lynton, up hill and down dale. If they had to go down the old coach road from Caffyn's to Lynton, they would have had to get out to lighten the vehicle, because the gradient was so steep. If they went straight up past Bratton Fleming, they came to Blackmoor Gate and Parracombe – and there was no bypass round Parracombe either in those days. Down and up another one-in-four hill. It must have been some journey; getting there at all was an achievement and an adventure.

Dinner must indeed have been 'eaten under the shadow of Castle Rock' with a great deal of relish, pick and choose or no pick and choose. If the picnic hamper was stowed between the knees of the boys on the cart, it might have been a surprise to find any sandwiches still left when they reached the Castle Rock.

Nevertheless, despite the rocks and the rolls, and the hours cramped together, they had a smashing time, and 'a very happy day was spent'. Well, consider the alternative.

Finally, the weather was 'very fine'. Is this yet another example of the great truth that Things Are Not What They Used To Be? Only this week I was told, for example, that the Headmaster of the Prep. School has had to postpone the school photograph no fewer than four times because of the weather – and this is the summer term. Those boys went in the Michaelmas holidays, at the beginning of October.

And, as a postscript, how about this as an idea for entertaining some of our foreign pupils who are forced to spend the Whitsun break here? Pack a hamper with wholesome sandwiches and ginger beer, hire a coach and horses from Arlington Court, squeeze in as many kids as possible, take away their Walkmans and Nintendos and portable CD players and mobile 'phones, and bounce them along 'B' and 'C' roads all the way to Lynton for a 'pic-nic'. Would they, I wonder, spend 'a very happy day'?

The main classroom in the original buildings – what was called 'Big School'.

The earliest known School photograph, from 1874. Look at the extraordinary variety of headgear.

A Glimmer of Equality

The *Register* of Midsummer, 1875 informed us that in the Oxford Local Examinations which began on 24 May of that year, there were 1871 candidates, who took their tests in Oxford, London, Bath, Birmingham, Boston, Brighton, Cheltenham, Gloucester, Hastings, Leeds, Leicester, Lincoln, Liverpool, Manchester, Margate, Nottingham, Rochester, Salisbury, Southampton, Southwark, Streatham Hill, Swansea, Taunton, Truro, Watford, West Buckland, Windermere and Wrexham. [Nice to see WB in the company of Birmingham, Liverpool and Manchester.]

Of those 1871 candidates, 411 were girls. Which seems to give the lie to the oft-repeated idea that nobody cared about girls' education till the turn of the century, or even after.

Blaming the Primary Schools

A conference of the middle-class 'county' schools was held in London, on 22 and 23 December 1873, attended by the heads of City of London School (the hosts), Hurstpierpoint, Framlingham, Whitgift, Bloxham, Cranleigh, Ardingly, Bedford and the county schools of Dorset and Devon (the D.C.S. – West Buckland).

The assembled headmasters adopted a minute which deplored the varying, and often very low, standards of the pupils coming to them from the various 'feeder' primary schools around them. 'Some are far advanced in one subject and some in another, while whole branches of necessary study have often been left untouched; and in a large number of cases, boys nine, or even eleven years old are sent to us, who cannot write or spell, or even read passably.'

[In other words, how could they be expected to make silk purses out of sows' ears? Now, where have we heard that before?]

They thought it might be useful to declare to these primary schools exactly what subjects were studied in the county schools, so that the primary heads could devise appropriate curricula and establish sufficient standards to enable their pupils to 'take a suitable place in the [county] school at the outset'. The subjects 'studied in all our schools are – 1. English grammar, with a work of some English author; 2. History and Geography; 3. French; 4. Arithmetic. The lower boys also learn writing and spelling; and in the schools higher mathematics are taught, in most Latin, in some German, Greek, and Physical Science'.

While they did not expect the primaries to excel in all these subjects, they did expect of a boy '1st, that he should be able to read intelligently, to write a clear, round hand, and to spell with tolerable correctness, for, till these are acquired he will hardly be able to receive lessons in classes with profit; and secondly, that his knowledge of English and literature, history, and geography, and as far as possible of French and Latin, should be on something like the same level.'

[Difficult to argue with that, though it was perhaps asking a lot for the primaries to teach French and Latin.]

✸ But Never Serious ✸

By the time the millennium came round, the School had been in existence for 142 years, and had been ruled by a total of fifteen headmasters. A simple sum will indicate that the average tenure of office, therefore, was a little under nine and half years. But, like most statistics, this can be misleading, because, of those fifteen, six held office for less than five years each. And, of those six, three sat in the headmaster's chair for less than two each.

These facts would seem to be evidence of some trouble somewhere, and it is indeed true that the School has had its share of incidents and crises. I have no figures to show the extent to which the School crisis ratio parallels, or exceeds, that of other similar schools, but this is not meant to be a comparative study. I am concerned with the history of only one school, and the very fact that, after such a turnover, West Buckland School is still here is a fine testimony to its resilience. Perhaps it is something to do with the spartan surroundings in which it was conceived and reared, and which many of its surviving members bravely extol. Perhaps it shares a quality with Glenn Miller's band; it can go on and on regardless of who is waving the baton (or the cane).

It is curious too that, if you examine the events surrounding the changeover of leadership, you discover a very high coincidence of change of head-master and crisis. Now, naturally, as the headmaster is the chief agent of authority, any departure of such a key figure is bound to send shock waves through the school, as is the arrival of a new one. It is like losing a parent, or gaining a spouse; you don't know what's coming.

But there is more to it than that. I am not putting the hypothesis that a crisis always produces a new head-master, or that a new headmaster always precipitates a crisis. But it is nevertheless a fact that the arrival, or departure, of a headmaster has coincided with a crisis – ten times. This, as I suggested above, is curious. The best way of making this case is to offer the evidence. So here goes.

It is usually assumed that the first Head, J.H. Thompson, was in active office, continuously, for thirty years, from 1858 to 1888. Not so. There was a gap of four years. Thompson, apparently, was becoming increasingly aware that his qualification, that of diploma from a teacher training college, was not fashionable or formidable – not for a head. This is no reflection on his teaching or his rule, but it was a fact that nineteenth-century headmasters normally had degrees and dog-collars. Well, they did in the best

places. So here was a sort of crisis: if the fledgling moorland academy over which he presided was going to hold its head high (to coin a phrase) in the more exalted company in which it was beginning to move, it behoved its chief executive to do something about it.

So he did. In 1867, he entered Jesus College, Cambridge, as an undergraduate, at the age of thirty, and took a B.A. degree in Maths (with honours) in 1871. He was also ordained as a deacon, and got himself appointed as Curate at East Buckland Church (and, naturally, as Chaplain of the School). By the peculiar process that obtains at Cambridge, he proceeded to the degree of M.A. in 1875 (though, oddly, he did not take Priest's Orders until 1886). During this period, he left the running of the School in the hands of his Second Master. So the circumstances in which the Revd W. Watson became Headmaster may not have constituted a full-blown crisis, but the circumstances were, to say the least, unusual.

When Thompson returned, he continued without a break until 1888. Perhaps the phrase 'without a break' contains a key to the problem that supervened then. Thompson was a bachelor (he did not marry until he had left); he lived on the premises; the work was unremitting and unending. Think of the many duties that a man in his position had to contend with – administrative, financial, public, pastoral, educa-tional, recreational – with the slenderest of staff and a minimum of domestic help – out there, in the middle of nowhere, with the only transport to distant towns a horse and trap, and of course the railway three miles away – and not even that until 1871.

His health had already broken down in 1879 – 'financial troubles', the records say – and he had had to go abroad (another small 'crisis'?). It seems hardly credible that, in the face of his work load in the decade that followed, his health could have been totally built up again.

So it was not surprising that he, albeit with great reluctance, tendered his resignation in 1888. He had been Headmaster, at least in name, for thirty years (still a record), and he was only just turned fifty. If you look at the photographs of him in the 1880s, he looks older than his age. It seems quite likely that the School had simply used him up.

However, the trouble in 1888 ran deeper than one man's broken health. The biggest reason lay in farming, from where the School drew most of its pupils. The Great Agricultural Depression had set in – great enough for historians to accord capital letters to it. Cheap corn from the American prairies and cheap refrigerated meat from New Zealand had ruined English farmers. Life being what it is, and always has been, it never rains but it pours – in this case literally. The 1870s and 1880s saw a string of soaking wet summers, interspersed with some fearsome winters. One after another, Devon farmers found that they could not afford even the moderate fees that the Devon County School asked. Thompson, who had got the School's numbers up from its original three to 150 by 1876, then saw them fall steadily to the low sixties by 1888.

That was not all. Forster's great Education Act of 1870, while it had not made primary (or 'elementary', as they called it then) schooling universal, compulsory, or free, had nevertheless established the principle of state initiative in education. The new Board schools, while they may not have provided the opportunities which the Devon County School offered in vocational teaching or moral training or general 'education', did place before a huge range of parents, and for the first time, the chance of a sound training in the three Rs – and for considerably less cost. It would appear that, because of Mr Forster's pioneering piece of legislation, the School suffered a loss of pupils, particularly at the lower end of the age range.

Finally, the Revd Brereton, the founder, put his finger on the fact that other schools were following the example of the Devon County School. In other words, the very success of D.C.S. had called into being some rivals in the West Country, and the catchment area was not unlimited.

The ill health of the Headmaster, falling rolls, rival schools – crisis enough for the new Headmaster, Mr C.C.S. Bland, to face. He got the numbers up to about 90 by 1895, but it was not really enough. The School's capacity was over 150, and at 60% occupancy it was not financially viable. It came close to closure. The solution was to forgo the School's financial independence and apply for county grants for technical instruction – which meant taking some Devon County Council pupils. It worked. Indeed, the progress of the new pupils and Bland's success in raising the numbers got him noticed, and he went off to become Headmaster of Ripon Grammar School. Crisis Number Two.

It is a further irony that the very success of the third Headmaster, J.B. Challen, in meeting the challenge caused Crisis Number Three.

He was an exceptional sportsman – football for Wales and cricket for Somerset – and by all accounts a popular fellow, who in the next few years attracted many a compliment on his running of the School. Then, without any warning that survives in the record, he quarrelled with the 'directors', and left in 1899. What was worse, he left with two-thirds of the boys, whose parents wanted them to join him in his new school at Barnstaple.

The Deputy Head, Mr W.A. Knight, took over, with the roll at a low of 31. Thirty-one – in a school the capacity of which was as high, at a pinch, as a hundred and eighty. It must have echoed like a cathedral. How the School survived the next six years seems, in retrospect, little short of a miracle. Yet, to look at the School photographs of the period, you would never guess how close they were to the bailiffs, or rather how close the bailiffs were to them. The high starched collars, the mortar boards, the watches and chains, the polished boots, the theatrical Victorian immobility, the heavy moustaches, the blazers, the caps – the total dignity of it all. There is nothing worried or scruffy or apologetic about any of it. It is a supreme testimony to the enormous self-confidence of the Edwardian Age, the age during which the sun never set on the British Empire. To look at these pictures, you would never suspect there was any trouble. They saw no crisis; they admitted no crisis; they showed no crisis; so there was none. And they survived.

To Knight's credit, he did get the numbers back up to the seventies, but this was still far short of a healthy viability. This was reflected in the School's finances, which became so anaemic during this period that, in the end, they had to be rescued by a syndicate of Old Boys. But that helped only with the present, not the future.

The Board of Education did not enjoy the prospect of such an institution limping along like this for – what seemed – ever. On the other hand, the shareholders did not like the idea of their precious company being wound up, to say nothing of the educational pioneers being dismayed at the imminent failure of their great experiment. The Board of Education would not give recognition to a school which would not accept their new proposed constitution. The Devon County Council put in their two pennyworth, saying they were not willing to increase their grant money, and moreover intimating that, if they had to take it over, they were not very happy either about assuming responsibility for a set of buildings that were three-quarters empty. And the School had no idea how it was going to be able to go it alone.

It took a long time, but the solution in the end was for the School to become a sort of grant-aided independent school, with a board of governors instead of a board of directors, on which body the local authority was to have a majority presence. In the future the School's income was to be founded on fees instead of shares, plus of course the local authority grants.

Without going into any further detail, one can, without much trouble, or fear of contradiction, classify this situation as Crisis Number Four. Just in time for the Revd E.C. Harries to have something to cut his teeth on as Headmaster.

He became Head in 1907, and remained so until 1934. If there was a Golden Age in the history of the School, this would probably be it. His career became the stuff of legend; stories stuck to him like glue. And the School went from strength to strength. By any standards, he was a great headmaster.

And yet – and yet – the fact remains that when he retired, the numbers were going down. All right, so they had gone up enormously since 1907. But by 1934, they were on the decline again. Crisis Number Five.

It was not Harries' fault; it was the fault of another depression – the Slump of the early 1930s. Once again, parents found that they could not maintain the fee expenditure. It was left to Commander Westall, his successor, to get the numbers back up again. But when Westall left, barely more than four years later, war clouds were looming, and crises don't come much bigger than that. Number Six.

Within another year, not only had some of the staff joined up; the Headmaster himself, Mr H.D. Badger, had gone off to war. Crisis Number Seven. His successor, who was little more than a stop-gap, did not stop the gap for long – less than a year. Crisis Number Eight was serious enough for the Governors to do what governors traditionally do only in times of crisis – offer the Headship to the Deputy Head, in this case Mr S.E. Howells.

For eleven years the School was crisis-free, except for small matters like the War and post-war austerity and so on. Then Mr Howells died in office in 1952 – Crisis Number Nine. For a few months, the Governors had to ask an ex-Headmaster and Old Boy, Mr C. Wheeler, to hold the fort until a new man could be found.

So, at the end of 1952, Mr L.W. Stephens came to a situation which had been a trifle *mouvementé*, to say the least. By the time he retired in 1968, he could legitimately claim an impressive string of successes – rising rolls (except at the end), a stronger sixth form, greater academic success, a lot of new building, admission to the Headmasters' Conference, and so on.

But his departure sparked a series of what (in default of a full available record) one can only call unfortunate incidents. Among other things, it involved a rash of resignations – senior staff, governors, and the new Headmaster himself, the Revd G. Ridding. The fact that these things happened, and that he was reinstated, indicates that there must have been dispute and disagreement at the very highest level, and a lot of bruised feelings. As with the events of 1907, it is hard to see how the word 'crisis'

can be called unjustifiable. Crisis Number Ten.

In 1978, Mr Ridding handed over to Mr M. Downward, who in turn, in 1997, handed over to Mr J. Vick. These two transfers of power seem to be the only ones in the history of the School that were not fraught in some way. Unless, that is, some fresh evidence of intrigue, administrative dry rot, or educational malfeasance comes seeping out of the pipes in the next fifty years.

But let us not meet trouble half way, and let us be grateful that for the last twenty years or so, things have bowled along pretty jolly uneventfully – at what you might call only 0.01 on the Richter Crisis Scale.

And yet – ten crises in 142 years – one every fourteen. And we have now gone over twenty years without one. The Devil has been silent for a long time; does that mean that Hell is brewing? We hope not. One can be sure, however, of one thing. However much we plan to deal with crises, however vigilant we try to be, we know that trouble, if and when it comes, will come from only one direction – an unexpected one.

Will Mr Hague, the new Prime Minister, abolish state schools? Will some vengeful ex-sixth-former accomplish a massive hack into the School's computer records and siphon off forty per cent of the School's fee income? Will the School be forced by a judgement of the European Court to take its share of refugee children from Kosovo, Ethiopia, Mozambique, Ruanda, Nigeria, Bangladesh, Guatemala, Namibia, Timor and Afghanistan? Will they discover oil under the tennis courts? Will the Anti-Blood Sports lobby succeed in abolishing rugby? Will a grateful Arab sheikh parent donate ten million pounds to the School – so long as it returns to single-sex education?

We do not know. But we feel confident that, whatever happens, the School will cope – one way or another. After what it has been through, any one of the above, or worse, will be a doddle.

It is said that in Germany they describe the difference between Berliners and Viennese in the following way: 'In Berlin the situation is often serious, but rarely hopeless; in Vienna, the situation is always hopeless, but never serious.'

Certainly an air of *insouciance* is more engaging than one of worry. Or, to put it another way, a crisis a day keeps the receiver away.

REV. J. H. THOMPSON, M.A.
(1858—1888)

C. C. S. BLAND, ESQ., M.A.
(1888—1895)

THE SCHOOL.

J. B. CHALLEN, ESQ., M.A.
(1895—1899)

REV. E. C. HARRIES, M.A.
(Present Head Master)

A quartet of early Headmasters:
The Revd J.H. Thompson (1858-1888), appointed at the age of twenty-one.
C.C.S. Bland (1888-1895) left to become head of Ripon Grammar School.
J.B. Challen (1895-1900) took two-thirds of the pupils with him when he went.
The Revd E.C. Harries (1907-1934), 'Ernie', who lies buried in East Buckland churchyard.

W.A. Knight (1900-1907) and his staff.   Back: A. Taylor (1895-1929), C. Wheeler (1903-1905), G.C. Fry (1903-1911). Front: Not known, W.A. Knight, E.C. Harries, Second Master/Chaplain (1900-1904). This picture includes three W.B. Heads – Knight, Harries (1907-1934), Wheeler (1952).

The Revd Harries, in senior and statesmanlike mode.

Harries again. He enjoyed riding, and could be seen chivvying laggard boys on the 'Exmoor', from the comfort of the saddle.

Commander Westall (1934-1939), Harries' successor, with Speech Day regalia.

Mr H.D. Badger (1939-1941) left to join the forces.

'Sam' Howells (1941-1952), third from the left in the front row, who, as Senior Master, was invited to take over in the War after three previous Heads had departed in two years. He died in office.

Leslie Stephens (1952-1968), with his prefects, all with Phoenix ties.

The Revd George Ridding (1968-1978), who steered the School through a bad time.

Michael Downward (1978-1997) won acceptance into the Headmasters' Conference.

One of the regular events in the School's Athletic Sports in the early 1870s was throwing the hammer.

School Football in 1875

From the *Register* of Christmas, 1875:

'The principal School matches were:
October 6.– 1st half of the Alphabet v. 2nd. – A drawn game, each side obtaining a gaol [*sic*], kicked respectively by G. Hallifax and Mr Thomas [a master].

October 13. – 1st and 2nd Classes v. the Rest. – A drawn game, resulting in a gaol [*sic* again] each obtained by L.L. Taplin and Dabb respectively.

October 16. – Devon v. The World. – Resulted in favour of the World by two gaols [*sic* for the third time], kicked by Wilkinson and G. Hallifax.'

[It will be, I am sure, a source of great pride to Devonians to read, at a time when the England cricket side quail at the prospect of a match against, say, Zimbabwe, and the England football team nearly fail to qualify for the European Cup, that Devon could take on the World, and lose by a mere two 'gaols'.]

Boys Have Always Been Boys

In 1874, the Rural Dean confided to his report that the boys of Devon County School were defacing the seats in East Buckland Church. He felt it only right that the repairs should be paid for by the School.

It had also been noted, in 1864, that many slates had been broken on both sides of the roof – which was odd, because, only two years before the entire church, except for the tower, had been rebuilt (and enlarged for the benefit of the School). Dare one suspect that this was the result of the attention of some of the more irreligious and ungrateful elements in the School?

A MODEL PUPIL

On 12 May 1884, eleven thousand, six hundred and sixteen candidates presented themselves for the Mathematics Examination set by the Science and Art Department of the Committee of Her Majesty's Most Honourable Privy Council on Education. The examination was set at four levels, called 'stages' – 'First', 'Second', 'Third' and 'Honours'. Nine thousand, six hundred and sixty-three came up for the First, and presumably the lowest, Stage. One thousand, two hundred and one gained a First Class, and two thousand, seven hundred and seventy failed. Five thousand, six hundred and ninety-two gained a Second Class. One of those who passed at Second Class level was Frederick Adams.

He attended West Buckland School (or rather the Devon County School, as it was called then) from 1882 to 1884. His age was entered on his Maths Certificate as 'sixteen', which puts his date of birth at 1868, give or take a few months.

Incidentally, the name of the man who signed Fred Adams' certificate – it looks like 'Donnelly' – is followed by the title 'Colonel, R.E.' So the tradition of ex-officers of the Armed Forces obtaining later employment in fields related to education (look how many bursars are ex-officers, for instance) seems to be a venerable one.

Also in passing, the reverse of Fred's certificate informs the interested reader or parent that the Science and Art Department of the Committee on Education of Her Majesty's Privy Council held, annually, examinations in a very wide variety of subjects – like Building Construction, Naval Architecture, Theoretical Mechanics, Geology, Principles of Mining, Animal Physiology, Steam, Principles of Agriculture, Physiography and Hygiene – but, curiously, not in 'Science' or 'Art'.

We do not have Fred Adams' Maths exam. papers, but we do have all the papers from the Cambridge Local Examinations which he sat at the end of 1883, when he was fifteen. He began, on Monday, 17 December, with Religious Knowledge – or rather four separate papers, on the Old Testament, the Acts of the Apostles, the Catechism, and the Gospel of St Luke. Each of these lasted for an hour and a quarter, and, according to the printed timetable, each followed immediately upon the other. Five hours non-stop! Were these poor wretches not allowed a break for a sandwich, or even for the needs of nature – from two o'clock to seven o'clock? And it got dark early in December. How did they finish? By gaslight? By lamplight? Electricity was a long way from West Buckland in 1883. And there was no central heating either. Five hours in the gloom and the cold, and nothing to eat, to say nothing of all the usual candidate's nerves – enough to play havoc with anyone's bladder, one would have thought.

In these unhelpful circumstances, poor Fred had to bring his mind to bear on questions which invited him to translate two passages from Ancient Greek, or which asked him to 'explain the words "Article", "rehearse", "baptism", "grace", "pomps" and "lusts"'. [An odd postscript there.]

On Tuesday, 18 December he tackled Maths. Arithmetic for two and half hours in the morning, and Euclid for another two and a half in the afternoon. So at least he got a break this time. Question 2 in the Arithmetic Paper informed him (which I bet you didn't know) that 'the interest on the National Debt is eighteen shillings and ninepence per second'. It then jolted him from gaping disbelief into action by demanding that he calculate how much that worked out at for a whole year – of 365 days, just in case he thought 1883 was a leap year. The Euclid paper asked him, among other things, to 'describe, on the longest side of a given scalene triangle, a rhombus equal to the triangle', and to 'shew that similar polygons are to one another in the duplicate ratio of their homologous sides.' I should think he needed a lunch break to cope with all that.

There were two hurdles facing him on Wednesday, Geography for an hour and three-quarters in the morning, and English Grammar for an hour and a half in the afternoon. There was one Geography question which asked him to 'name, in order, the states on the left bank of the Mississippi, and [to] give the chief town of each'. How many Geography *teachers* could do that straight off the top of their head today? The English paper was full of the sort of questions about infinitives and prepositional phrases that you would expect, and which it is easy to sneer at for their pedantry in these more informal days.

Indeed, it is easy to sneer at a lot of the pedantry of the questions in most of the papers, but they reflect the times. One must remember that education in 1883 was still, on a national scale, in its infancy; the system then was not nation-wide; it was not compulsory; and it was not free. So-called educational experts had no long or wide experience to fall back on, so they relied on the assumptions about knowledge and children and citizenship that obtained at the time. A child should be brought up to be obedient, God-fearing, diligent, careful, accurate and neat. And not ignorant. Whatever else you may say about a child's education in the 1880s, it was not starved of factual information. ('Name all the states on the left bank of the Mississippi...'; 'Name with dates the chief battles between English and Scotch armies from the time of Edward I to the accession of James I' [that's from 1272 to 1603 – 331 years!].)

How often do we hear complaints today – from parents, teachers, employers, university tutors and so on – that today's young people are life-threateningly ignorant? And as for being brought up to be obedient, God-fearing, diligent, careful, accurate and neat – well, could even a modern crackpot educational reformer make a case against that? Certainly few parents would argue with it.

Of course, there are all sorts of other dimensions to the business of education now, which make the above questions not entirely fair. But one thing remains constant: whatever educational regime the adult world comes up with in its wisdom, it is the poor individual pupil who has to cope with it, make the best of it, and find his way through it or round it.

And our Frederick was very good at that. Several of his school reports survive, all of which testify to his good conduct and to his industry. In those days, the School Magazine, the *Register*, used to publish lists of boys who had good records for diligence and punctuality. Frederick Adams' name appeared in these lists during every term of his recorded attendance. More – there were four categories in the 'work' section: those who had had no complaints registered against them at all, those who had had only one complaint registered; those who had two, and those with three. Fred's name appeared regularly in the top group. Similarly, his name appeared every time in the list of boys who were 'never' late.

Proof of his diligence comes in his surviving exercise book, where, in beautiful figures, he successfully multiplied three thousand, seven hundred and sixty-one pounds, sixteen shillings and twopence-half-penny by four hundred and fifty-nine, and then divided six hundred and ninety-six thousand, four hundred and eighty-five pounds, two shillings and ninepence three-farthings by seven hundred and sixty-five, and got that right too. (Incidentally, the sign for a correct sum was not a tick, but an elaborate 'R'.)

And look at his maps. He may have had trouble remembering all those towns on the left bank of the Mississippi, but he could have reeled off the names of nearly forty rivers in North and Central America.

He does not appear, however, to have distinguished himself on the games field. No mention of his name figures in the voluminous reports, often accompanied with full scoresheets, of the School's cricket matches.

Nor was he a very good footballer, it seems. It is possible that he took part in the Exmoor runs, but no records of individual performances survive from that period, apart from the names of winners.

Two letters remain though, both written in beautiful copperplate, and both, judging from their tone, dictated by a teacher standing very nearby. One begins 'Dear Mother' (which may be genuine enough), but the other begins 'Dear Parent', which most certainly is not. The use of words like 'luncheon' and phrases like 'particularly requested' reveal the eagle eye of the vigilant master over the shoulder. Even allowing for the greater formality of letters in those days, it is difficult to see Fred ending a real letter home with the words 'I am, dear Parent, Yours Affectionately F. Adams'.

Interestingly, there also survive two or three envelopes, in which these semi-official letters were delivered. They measure only about five and a half inches by three; they are embossed, in minute letters, with the name and address of the manufacturers, just under the sealing flap: 'Partridge & Cooper, Makers, 192, Fleet Street'; and they bear on the back the name of the School, also in slight relief, and in red, old English script. A small, fairly new, remote and totally obscure boarding school for the sons of the middle class, stuck in the back of beyond, bought embossed stationery from Fleet Street.

In this spartan establishment, Frederick Adams spent two or more of the most formative years of his young life. He was quiet, diligent and careful. No great shakes out of the classroom. The Revd Thompson, the Headmaster, often found it difficult to say much about him: 'His conduct has been very good, and he has done his work very well'; 'his conduct is excellent, and he does his work very well'; 'his conduct has generally been very good, and he has been painstaking in his work'.

It could be, of course, that the Revd Thompson was not a very imaginative, or very industrious cleric, and that he wrote something like this about lots of pupils, but the picture that emerges of Fred is nevertheless that of an ordinary sort of boy who was not especially gifted in any direction, and who kept his nose clean and his head down. Like thousands of others over the years. Quiet lads who did their best. And they went on, most of them, to do their best in adult life as well, in whatever situation a wayward Fate placed before them – working in an office, making ends meet, raising a family, dying in a war.

We do not know what Fred thought about his teachers, his school, his friends (if he had any), his future. We have no idea what pleased him, what angered him (difficult to imagine Fred in a temper), what worried him, what distressed him. What did he want to do? What did he want to be?

How many Fred Adams' went through the School? Hundreds and thousands, probably. Like the 'those there be' in Ecclesiastes, 'who have become as if they had never been'. But, like those in Ecclesiastes, their name does live 'for evermore', because they built the bedrock of the School, like the millions of crustaceans whose remains built cliffs. The prodigies, the geniuses, the gilded ones – of course their light shone forth, and that is as it should be. They were the stars, and every institution needs its stars. But the others –

the ordinary majority – who have just as many solid virtues as their more gifted schoolmates (often more) – they are the ones who provide the mirror in which the light of the stars is reflected and magnified.

And how many of us would be more than content to see on our gravestone 'his conduct has been excellent and he has done his work very well'?

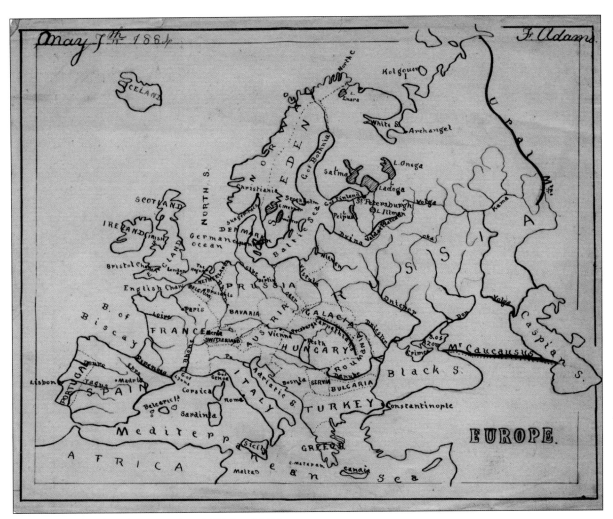

One of Fred Adams' maps, dated 7 May 1884.

The Masters and Monitors, 1881.
Back row: l. to r: H.H. Taplin, A.E. Butt, T. Stone (master), R.R. Luxton. Middle row: all the remainder standing, l. to r: C.G. Rogers, L.T. Oakley, F.H. White, R.P. Chope, E.C. Pierce, A.E.P. Hughes, T.R. Potbury, F.A. Coon, L.H. Farrington.   Front row: l. to r: W. Thomas (master), R.M. Latham (master), J.H. Thompson (H.M.), J.G. Shain (master), P. Gross (master), W.E. Calvert (master).

The Masters and Monitors, 1884.
Back row: l. to r. C.C. Percy, J.A. Chope, F.G. Cundall, A. Watts, S.H. Bradford, W.G. Allen, F.W. Gates, A.J. Tucker, A.A. Little. Front row: J.G. Shain, T.R. Potbury, R.M. Latham, J.H. Thompson, W.E. Calvert, W.H. Bennett, W. Thomas. (All except Potbury in the front row are masters.) Look at the bowler hats and watch chains, among the boys! It does not say that A.J. Tucker is a master, so we have a pupil with a fine moustache. And the poses. It is a long way from the hands-on-knees, rigid uniformity of modern group photos.

A Very Warm Friend

The *Register* of Christmas, 1882, recorded the sad news that the Revd J. Hallifax, M.A., Rector of Breane, Somerset, had died on 8 November of that year. He was, the magazine remarked, 'a warm friend of the School, no less than eight of his sons having been educated as boarders in it'.

Lower down the page came the sadder news that Octavius Hallifax, son of the above, had been killed at Dutoitspan, in South Africa, aged only twenty. This had happened on 3 October.

[It seems quite likely, does it not, that the two events are not unconnected.]

How to Kill a Contest

Early on in my researches in the Archive, I came across a photograph of a scene from Shakespeare – a photograph, no less, of the famous 'pound of flesh' scene from *The Merchant of Venice*. It was dated 1881, and this was confirmed by the survival of the original playbill of the production at the School. And the picture, like so many I have come across from the School's early days, was in surprisingly good nick.

I wondered whether this represented the very first performance of the Bard on Exmoor, and offered the piece for publication in the local press. Had it, I mused, been anticipated by a production of *Hamlet* in 1664 at Heasley Mill to celebrate the Bard's centenary? Or had there been a performance of *Henry V* in the open air at Dunkery as a loyal offering to the newly-crowned George III in 1760? Or did they do *Romeo and Juliet* to mark the wedding of Queen Victoria to Prince Albert? And so on.

The local paper not only printed the piece, but issued a sort of challenge. It was taken up. We were soon informed, in the pages of the *North Devon Journal*, that there had been just such a performance, at South Molton, of *Macbeth*, in 1834. And they still had the playbill to prove it. Indeed, the George inn, where it was put on, had been formerly known as *The Globe*.

The paper was obviously quite tickled with this story, and hoped it would go on running: 'If you know of an earlier Shakespeare production in North Devon, let us know.'

Somebody did. A local historian. He claimed documentary evidence that there had been a visit to Bideford as early as 1605, by the Bard himself.

[Which is as good a way of killing a competition as one could devise.]

HOW ROSY ARE THE SPECTACLES

Nineteenth-century clergymen, it seems, were given to publishing their sermons. Well, some of them anyway. The printed record of the events and happenings of the Devon County School, in its early days, is sprinkled with slender folders, or discreet inserts, of printed sermons, by resident or visiting or celebrity clerics, or, sometimes, of speeches by V.I.Ps.

The first Headmaster, the Revd J.H. Thompson, went in for this. Round about 1881 (because he refers to 'looking back on the history of the twenty-two or nearly twenty-three years of the life of this School'), he paused half-way through one sermon to muse on the sort of boy he and the School were turning out.

'If one could fix at one's wish the character a West Buckland boy [note – 'West Buckland', not 'Devon County School' – a Freudian slip? An unconsciously prophetic utterance from a man of the cloth?] should bear in the world, one would express the hope and the prayer that he might be brave yet gentle, manly and yet modest – open-hearted, industrious, and with true and deep Christian feeling. And many and many a boy has well deserved the character.'

Well, you may think, he would say that, wouldn't he? Yes, he probably would. He was a man of the nineteenth century; he was a clergyman; and he was the headmaster of a pioneering school who was keen to make the point that the great experiment entered upon by Brereton and Fortescue and himself was working. And if his sermon was going to be read by legions of Old Boys, whose memories became more fond and misty with each passing year, he was preaching to the converted. After all, he was paying them all a compliment; of course they would agree with him.

True, true, and true again.

Was there anything in it, then? Was there anything in what he said which might carry any weight with a more perceptive posterity?

One thing which strikes the reader is the use of some nice words which have now slipped mostly out of use. 'Manly' may not be common parlance now; it may even raise a smile of tolerant amusement. But it is a good word; it conveys the combined virtues of masculinity, self-respect, courtesy and capacity for compassion rather neatly. It even sounds better than 'macho' or 'Rambo'. Then again, 'open-hearted' does not often get an airing, but it deserves to. It carries with it an impression of generosity and good fellowship and innocent charm without *naiveté* or beery matiness.

Consider too Thompson's discretion. For all that he was a clergyman, and a Victorian clergyman at that, he did not thrust the Bible down his listeners' throats. Note that he did not say that Christian faith was the hallmark of the West Buckland boy. No – it was 'Christian feeling'. That conveys the genuine charity and common sense kindness of Christ's Samaritan far better than the 'faith' of a Pharisaic conformist.

So – if you can cut through the manners and language habits of the day, it may be that Thompson had something to offer this century as well. Now consider what he went on to say.

'Some three or four years ago a clergyman, well known to most of us, was travelling in a railway train [I like that – not 'train', but 'railway train'], when in a conversation that arose the name of the West Buckland School was mentioned. A young man joined in the conversation. He was, he said, for some two or three years at West Buckland School. And, he said, there was one noble thing about that School, that he had often thought of since he had left and seen something of the world, and that was that a boy, if there was anything in him, could always make his own way in the School: there was that gentlemanly feeling in the School that prevented a boy's ever being sneered at because of his father's occupation or his father's religion. A boy depended on himself, on his own good feeling and good sense, and was never subjected to the sneers of those who either were, or believed themselves to be, socially his superiors.

'I do not know who the old boy was that gave among strangers that character to his old School, but the gentleman who related the anecdote, and who did not know or ask the old boy's name, said he should tell it again and again as a noble testimony to the manliness and gentlemanliness of West Buckland boys. A boy at this School depended for his position on himself – not on favouritism, not on the social position of his friends, but on his own industry, his own good manners, his own right feeling and his own good sense.'

Notice how Thompson repeated the main sentiments at the end. He was enough of a professional preacher to hammer in a good moral when he found one.

Now – how will that story go down with readers who survived four or six or nine years or whatever of the twentieth-century West Buckland? Will they remember being ignored for being weedy and totally unsuitable for the lion-hearted First Fifteen? Will the dread of heart-bursting cross-country runs fill their memories? Do they still carry the scars of bullying? Do any of them recall discrimination because their family was Catholic? Maybe.

But were they in a majority or a minority? Were their cases sufficiently rare for Thompson's generalisations to stand up? After all, remember that Brereton's vision was of a school for the *middle*-class. By definition that implied there was to be no social discrimination between those well born and those below them. If anyone wanted a 'toff' education, let them go to a posh public school; there were enough of them. And there was little or no danger of a working-class boy being victimised because there were no children of the slums or tenements or back-to-backs involved, or very, very few, for the simple reasons that they could not afford the fees and did not live close enough. (It is no good the socialists getting hot under the collar about Brereton's snobbery. In mid-Victorian England, it was a major triumph that reformers were getting to grips at last with *middle*-class education, never mind education for all. His foundation in 1858 was twelve years ahead of Forster's great Education Act; nor did that provide a universal education even at primary level, and it certainly did not make education free, much less compulsory.)

Another of Brereton's ideas was to get away from a strictly denominational regime. One has only to glance at the bitter wrangling that went on in Victorian England about the place of religion in education – every major education law was fought tooth and nail, largely over religion – to realise that this was a truly pioneering concept.

And note that that old boy in the train made the proviso that any boy could make his way 'if there was anything in him'. If one is teased, for instance, the best way to cure it is to find one's own way of dealing with it; there is no infallible way of legislating against bullying. As Martin Luther King is supposed to have said, 'You can only ride on a man's back if it is bent.' The success has to come from inside first. No matter what type of school it is, the boy has first to say to himself something like 'Right! I'll bloody well show you'.

The debate, as they say, can continue. Just what were the old school days really like? Were they really the repositories of those great, timeless, rock-bottom virtues that one would like to think were there? Does our affection iron away the creases of the faults? If it does, something must have put the affection there.

I don't know. But, just as a postscript, may I refer you to the piece entitled 'A Typical Product'. Notice how close Ted Woodman's virtues came to those recorded by Thompson. And there is over a century between them. Can it be that there really is something in what Thompson said?

One of the commonest sights in any secondary classroom up and down the country. This type of desk lasted for years and years – and years.

The old Manual Workshop (1914), later turned into the Marshall Dormitory.

Cleanliness may have been next to godliness, but it is difficult to escape the impression that a medieval monastery had better ablutions that this. And what did the ladders have to do with it?

Making A Meal Of It

An Old Boys' cricket day today is what it says – a day. Go to a Past v. Present cricket match in the 1880s, and you would not get away for four days.

In 1885, Old Boys began to arrrive on Thursday, 6 August. A report of the event has survived – specially printed, six pages. Four of those six were devoted to the cricket match. The report was almost a ball-by-ball commentary. It recorded every fall of every wicket, every change of bowling, every noteworthy incident. There were two innings on each side, and a full scorecard was printed too, complete with bowling analysis.

No fewer than six members of the Taplin family played, one in the School side and five in the Old Boys'. There was a very relaxed attitude to the clock. For instance, the game did not start till 12.45 on the Friday, and went on until the School first innings closed at 2.40. Lunch took an hour and twenty minutes. But on Saturday, play began at 10.40. The Old Boys' first innings closed at eleven, when a photographer took pictures of the two teams. At 11.30 the School second innings began, and lasted until 1.50. Lunch took an hour and fifty minutes. The Old Boys lost by just ten runs.

Amongst the features of the cricket were three hits for five, including one that 'went past the new pavilion and half way across the field behind'. So it seems likely that there were no boundaries; everything had to be run. Which makes F.O. Taylor's hit for six seem prodigious. In the Old Boys' second innings Mr Thomas 'went on to bowl slow underhands', and got a wicket. The scorecard also records that Thomas bowled a no-ball, which, if he was bowling 'slow underhands', must have been quite a feat.

On the Friday evening, there was a 'Dramatic Entertainment', in which four of the cast were in the School team. Busy lads. On the Saturday evening, all the Old Boys attended a formal dinner in the Dining Hall. So did the entire School. Speeches were made, toasts drunk, songs sung. There was 'great cheering'. At the end, the 'whole party adjourned to the quadrangle, which had been lit up by a large number of Chinese lanterns'. They stood round the Archbishop's tree and sang 'Auld Lang Syne'.

On Sunday there were two services. At the end of the second 'all joined in singing the Hymn for Old Boys' Sunday, written for these gatherings at the School by the Rev. S. Childs Clarke, Vicar of Thorverton'. (I wonder how many people know it now.)

❉ Nails Aren't What They ❉ Used To Be

For the first time I now know what it's like to be an archaeologist.

Many years ago I read a book called *Digging up the Past*. It was written by Sir Leonard Woolley, one of the early-twentieth-century pioneers of British archaeology. I believe he made his reputation in Mesopotamia, where once flourished the ancient civilisation of Babylon and Sumeria.

This chap Woolley was the first person to get across to me that archaeology is not a matter of poncing about in a pith helmet and discovering lost civilisations by Friday afternoon; it is about time, and patience, and dirt, and heat, and dust, and clearing away mountains with teaspoons and toothbrushes so that you don't miss anything.

True, one of the very first archaeologists, Heinrich Schliemann, did ponce about in a pith helmet and he did discover the civilisation of Troy practically single-handed, and a lot of priceless gold jewellery too. But he was, by modern standards, a butcher. He missed, or destroyed, a great deal as he hacked his way down to the treasure of (as he thought) King Priam and the jewels of Helen of Troy.

I got a whiff of all this today when I took some old photographs out of their frames. Yes, the pleasure and interest – the jewels of Helen bit – were there. One gazed in patronising amusement at the stolid faces of football teams from the 1890s, or the lofty glances askance of a group of schoolmasters from the Edwardian era. Ho-ho! Look at the stiff collars and the enormous moustaches and the watches and chains. And the funny little caps on the boys, and their unbelievable football boots.

But when you turn the pictures over in order to extract them from the frames, then – then – you discover what Sir Leonard was on about – the dirt, the dust, the stains on the glass, the crumbling cardboard backing, the rusting hanging brackets, the brittle tacks.

I never thought I would be affected by the thought, as I peeled off the frayed paper covering of the back, that I was the first person to touch this for a hundred years. On the backs of some of the photographs someone had written, in beautiful copperplate, the relevant date – 1910, 1912, or whatever. There it was – never seen the light of day for over eighty years. Two world wars had come and gone since that had been written. On the paper covering at the back the photographic firm had stuck a label of their trade plate. 'Elliott and Fry – Artists – 55, Baker Street, Portman Sq. London, W.1.' And it wasn't just your computer printing; it was done out with the most beautiful scroll work – a piece of art in itself. You wanted to rush to a telephone directory to see if they're still there.

When I prised off a piece of plywood backing, a tiny circle of knotwood fell away from the parent board. As if it had been waiting ninety years to have the freedom to do it. Like a genie let out of a bottle. It made it almost alive. You could imagine it sighing with relief to be able to relax at last.

As I freed more and more football teams and cadet corps and common room members from their stained and mottled glass prisons and looked at their faces direct, as you might say, I was surprised to see how well the actual prints had stood up to the years. Then I found myself beginning to compare. Not the photographs. The backings. Woolley's teaspoon and toothbrush again.

Some nails were easy to extract from the back of the frame. Some simply snapped almost with finger pressure. Some had to be wrenched out like deep-set molars from a dotard's gum. Some pictures were backed, as I said, with plywood. Some with cardboard. Some glazing was thick; some was thin. I wondered whether glass deteriorated with time. Does glass, like metal, suffer from molecular fatigue? (Which, incidentally, added a further dimension, that of danger, to the process.)

Then I began to wonder – was there any reason why some photo-frames and mountings and backings were, frankly, better done than others? Even the wood seemed to vary. Had Messrs Elliott and Fry gone into decline? Did they fall under new management? You know – only interested in profit, no regard for the old skills, content with a half-done job.

Or did it run deeper than that?

I noticed that the framings that had come from just before the First World War seemed more thoroughly finished than those which came after it. Plywood. Stronger nails. Thicker glass. Whereas those from 1919 were backed by cheap cardboard. And the tacks practically fell out – those that did not snap when you grasped them with a pair of pliers. Is it too fanciful to guess that after four years of hardship and privation and national loss, standards, of both supplies and workmanship, had slipped? Going back further, to the period of greatest assurance in the 1890s, when the sun never set on the British Empire, the framing of the football team of 1895 is so robustly put together – it is such a thorough job – involving actual screws as well as tacks, and a proper piece of wood panel backing instead of plywood – that I have not yet been able to take it to bits.

If you doubt the impact of the First World War as apparently indicated by the mere backing of a batch of framings and mountings, you have only to turn them over and look at the faces. Of the staff. In six years, under normal circumstances, you would not expect faces to change much. But compare the staff of 1913 with that of 1919. Two in particular – senior men who were in both pictures. Hair and moustaches have

gone from black, or at best grizzled, to grey, even with white streaks. Wisps of hair on one scalp have given way to reveal a dome. And it would not take much imagination to deduce that they looked sadder. As well they might.

Just as archaeologists delve into middens as well as into treasure chests to probe the secrets of a civilisation, so I felt I had gained a faint insight into the desolation caused by the First World War, not only by gazing on long-dead faces, but by tugging at rusty nails and rotten cardboard.

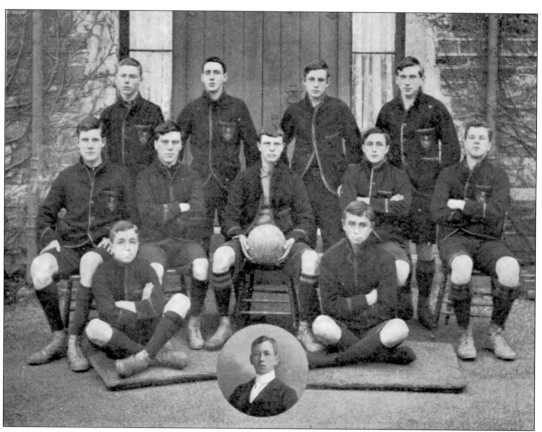

The 'Devon County School Football Team, 1903-04', who got themselves into the pages of the magazine *Health and Strength* in 1907. There was an article about the School too, and about the bracing effects of the Devon air on young sportsmen.

W.A. Knight and his School, very early in the century. When Knight took over, the numbers had fallen as low as 31. He got them up to the seventies.

The School in 1904 (we know that Harries left in 1904 and Fry came in Dec., 1903, and they are both here).

The School Staff and prefects in 1913. There cannot be many school staff photos in which the Headmaster's mother figures so prominently. (Harries did not marry till 1918, when he was fifty.)

The School Staff and prefects in 1919. Note some changes. First, the presence of female staff. Second, the appearance of S.M. Howells (extreme left, front row), later Senior Master and finally Headmaster. Finally, look at Harries, and at Taylor, on Harries' left as you look at them in both pictures. Compare their pictures in 1913, and see what those years of war and strain had done to them, particularly Taylor.

Two pages from the Reading and Debating Society's debate on Women's Suffrage in 1906.

The Ladies – God Bless 'Em

The School Reading and Debating Society was set up in 1903, and was the ancestor of the Phoenix Society. Among many thorny contemporary topics it debated or read papers about were hunting, the Boer War, the Yellow Peril, a Channel tunnel, and votes for women.

In the women's suffrage debate of 1906, one chauvinist was allowed to get away with the observation that 'women interruptions at election meetings are very frequent and that he thought that at every hall a mouse should be kept which could be let loose if necessary'.

Another speaker offered the odd theory that 'the only reason why women should be given votes was that they made good spies.'

[Pick the bones out of that.]

The Detective Schoolmaster

A teacher from nearly a hundred years ago was credited with being able to identify which boys in the class had been smoking on autumn mornings before school. He simply looked at their boots. If they were covered with dew, he knew that their owners had been up in one of the fields behind a hedge. Elementary!

They Don't Do Dinners Like That Any More

The Edwardians, they say, were great eaters. This is amply borne out by the dinner they bore in for the Devon County School Old Boys' Association at the Holborn Restaurant on Friday, 11 January 1907. Not West Buckland – Devon County School. And the pupils and Old Boys were very proud of it and of its strong traditions, which already, by 1907, were nearly half a century old.

How many schools then or now, for instance, could boast or have boasted, that they had as one of their guests their first Headmaster from forty-nine years before? But the Revd J.H. Thompson, M.A., was there, and, from his photograph on the front cover of the menu, looking fit and sharp.

How many Old Boys' Associations bother now to produce for the occasion, or can afford to produce, a souvenir menu-programme on four stiff pages, in two-tone colour, with proper photographs on front and back?

How many Old Boys' Associations nowadays can claim to have sat down to a meal of eight separate courses? How many Old Boys' Associations can assume enough command of French among their members to have every item on the menu printed in that language – without an English translation in brackets underneath?

Do you want to know what they had to eat? I translate – just in case. 'Crust in the pot, with ruby cream.' 'Ruby cream'? Sounds like a pop group. 'Creamed turbot Alexandra' – no doubt after Edward VII's Danish Queen. More fish to follow – whitebait. Whitebait, too humble to be named after anybody.

Then – the intestines having been primed, as you might say – saddle of mutton and redcurrant jelly, cauliflower with grated cheese, and potatoes. Well, actually *pommes boulangère* – so, presumably potatoes done specially by the baker's wife. Enough meat? No. You had to tuck in next to braised ham and spinach. And you still were not let off, because there was turkey casserole and salad to follow.

You were then faced with a sort of culinary obstacle course, in the shape of *pouding Saxon* – no doubt a worthy Teutonic stodge; *glace plombière* – which sounds like ice cream made by the plumber's wife, but which is actually *tutti-frutti*, because I looked it up; and vanilla wafers. No choice. That was it – all on one dish. And that was not the dessert. 'Dessert' was announced below as a completely separate item – its actual details kept a secret as a treat for eager digestions or as a punishment for delicate ones.

In case you're thinking that things aren't what they used to be and that you'd like to have been there, there is a curious absence of any mention of wine. So perhaps it's not so bad these days after all. There is always the possibility, of course – because, as you can see, they did things properly then – that there was an individual wine menu that has not come down to us. Imagine – a fresh wine for each course. In Edwardian times, only too likely.

Their stamina must have been Olympian, because the evening had only just begun at the Holborn Restaurant. After the 'Menu' came the 'Programme'.

Twenty-three separate items, beginning with the loyal toast, and ending with 'Auld Lang Syne'. So many, in fact, that there was even a printed 'Interval'.

Almost every item deserves quoting, but we must choose only the very best. For example, there was a performance of the 'Song of the Devon County School' – 'Hail to the School' – sung by Mr Emile d'Oisly (words by the Revd J.L. Brereton, music by Mr. Hubert Bath) and accompanied by the composer. No fewer than nine other songs were performed during the course of the evening.

The titles of some of the songs make the imagination fairly take flight. How about 'Father O'Flynn'? Did he have the sort of adventures that befell his Hollywood namesake? 'Gipsy John'? Was this a decorous, euphemistic, male version of Eskimo Nell? Or 'Richard of Taunton Deane'? The exploits of an Edwardian resident at a West Country service station? Or 'My Inquisitive Kiddie'? What, one wonders, was he inquisitive about? And believe it or not, later in the programme, the last song but one, was 'Queer Questions'.

Visiting dignitaries had to sing for their supper – in some cases quite literally. The old Headmaster, the Revd Thompson, had to make one of the replies to the toasts – of which there were five. And the newly-appointed Headmaster, the Revd Harries, B.A., had to sing the aforesaid 'Richard of Taunton Deane'. No doubt later headmasters fresh to their post have had cause to be grateful that this practice did not become a firm tradition at Old Members' Dinners.

The Old Boys finally tottered out into the winter small hours in Holborn, oozing nostalgia, cigar smoke, and the last outrageous verse of 'Gipsy John'. Pity the horses and cab drivers who had to carry them back to their hotels.

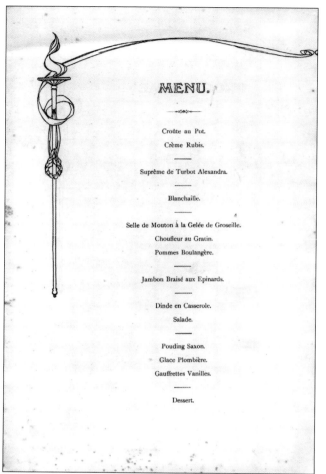

MENU.

Croûte au Pot.

Crème Rubis.

Suprême de Turbot Alexandra.

Blanchaille.

Selle de Mouton à la Gelée de Groseille.

Choufleur au Gratin.

Pommes Boulangère.

Jambon Braisé aux Epinards.

Dinde en Casserole.

Salade.

Pouding Saxon.

Glace Plombière.

Gauffrettes Vanilles.

Dessert.

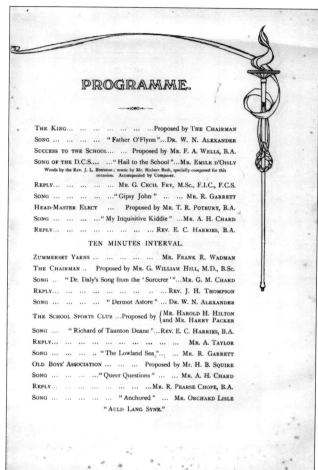

PROGRAMME.

THE KING...	...Proposed by THE CHAIRMAN
SONG	"Father O'Flynn"...DR. W. N. ALEXANDER
SUCCESS TO THE SCHOOL... ...	Proposed by MR. F. A. WELLS, B.A.
SONG OF THE D.C.S. ...	"Hail to the School"...MR. EMILE D'OISLY

Words by the Rev. J. L. Brereton; music by Mr. Hubert Bath, specially composed for this occasion. Accompanied by Composer.

REPLY...	MR. G. CECIL FRY, M.Sc., F.I.C., F.C.S.
SONG	..."Gipsy John" ... ... MR. R. GARRETT
HEAD-MASTER ELECT ...	Proposed by MR. T. R. POTBURY, B.A.
SONG	..."My Inquisitive Kiddie" ...MR. A. H. CHARD
REPLY...	... REV. E. C. HARRIES, B.A.

TEN MINUTES INTERVAL.

ZUMMERSET YARNS	MR. FRANK R. WADMAN
THE CHAIRMAN ..	Proposed by MR. G. WILLIAM HILL, M.D., B.Sc.
SONG .. "Dr. Daly's Song from the 'Sorcerer'"...MR. G. M. CHARD	
REPLY...	... REV. J. H. THOMPSON
SONG	"Dermot Astore" ... DR. W. N. ALEXANDER
THE SCHOOL SPORTS CLUB ...Proposed by { MR. HAROLD H. HILTON and MR. HARRY PACKER	
SONG ... "Richard of Taunton Deane"...REV. E. C. HARRIES, B.A.	
REPLY...	MR. A. TAYLOR
SONG ... ... "The Lowland Sea"... ... MR. R. GARRETT	
OLD BOYS' ASSOCIATION	Proposed by MR. H. B. SQUIRE
SONG ... ..."Queer Questions " ... ... MR. A. H. CHARD	
REPLY...	...MR. R. PEARSE CHOPE, B.A.
SONG	"Anchored" ... MR. ORCHARD LISLE

"AULD LANG SYNE."

A Menu and Programme for the Devon County School Old Boys' Association annual dinner in January, 1907. There were eight courses, ten speeches, and ten songs.

In a speech to the Old Boys, the ex-Headmaster, Mr J.B. Challen, recalled a cricket match that he had played in during the 1890s, in which, after a 10.30 start, West Buckland (no doubt stiffened with masters, including himself) 'put 300 runs on the board before lunch for five or six wickets – a thing he never remembered having seen either before or since'.

THE JUBILEE YEAR

In 1908, the School celebrated its first fifty years. On Monday, 27 July of that year, the boat was duly pushed out – a star-studded Prize Day, and the first dramatic effort for many years involving the Bard. Celebrity and culture were to be the ingredients for a memorable day. No effort was to be spared to make the journey from Barnstaple, South Molton and Bratton Fleming (not to mention London) worthwhile for the visitors.

It would have been interesting to know how those visitors made the trip from their respective towns and villages – by dog-cart, horse-bus, train (at least to Filleigh), and by the new-fangled motor car. Did any intrepid travellers do it on a bicycle? Did any tough farmers' wives walk in their best finery over Leary Hill? Did any ride? And who looked after all these myriad forms of transport when they arrived?

Guests were certainly greeted hospitably; everybody was treated to 'an informal luncheon'. The *North Devon Journal* tells us so, in a reprinted report ('with additions and corrections' – so it would appear that the *Journal* was getting it wrong in 1908 as well) that ran to eight or nine pages in the School magazine.

Having, as the Victorians would have put it, 'fortified the inner man', the School authorities then proceeded to lift up the spirit, with a performance of 'some scenes' from *As You Like It*. Some optimist on the staff – a keen young English teacher from the Home Counties? – took the daring chance of presenting it in the open air. In North Devon, on Exmoor, in July. He had apparently found a very convenient and 'admirable forest glade' quite close to the School, and there a handful of boys, got up in costumes hired all the way from London, recited their lines (most of them anyway), and did their best not to trip over hems and scabbards and tussocks of grass. A photograph of this Thespian Fifteen (is it entirely coincidence that they numbered the same as a rugby team?) still survives, in surprisingly good condition.

It is possible that the idea for this production was put in the mind of that putative keen young English teacher by a visit paid to the School the previous autumn by a Mr H. Stanford Webber. This gentleman had given a 'Dramatic Recital', Part One of which was taken up with 'Scenes from *As You Like It*'. The School magazine reported that it had been 'intensely enjoyed both by the School and by a considerable number of visitors'. As is well known, you can't keep scruffy, philistine, fourteen-year-old boys away from Shakespeare, and there is nothing an Exmoor farmer

and his wife like better as a relief from the milking than a dose of blank verse.

It is such a pleasure, in these dismal days when we deplore the fact that the only thing the great British public wants is more soap operas, to be told by the *Journal* that the School's performance (or the Thespian Fifteen forward and back play) was much enjoyed by the Prize Day visitors, who were both 'appreciative' and 'generous'. (Perhaps a tiny sliver of realism is gently inserted by the use of the word 'generous'.)

The *Journal* critic was also honest enough to point out that 'many of the characters spoke too fast', and that Rosalind 'did not know his part thoroughly'. Note 'his'. (I bet M.R. Roberts got a wigging for that afterwards, when the last of the open motor cars had spluttered their way back over Leary Hill *en route* to the more familiar and congenial delights of the public bar at the *George* in South Molton.) Phoebe, said the critic, 'looked charming', but then she would; the boy who played her, L.G.H. Major, went up later in the day to receive the School Divinity Prize. And William was 'nearly perfect'. (Bully for A.P. Moor, who later snaffled the Form Four Maths Prize.) And – a final bouquet that displayed the critic's generosity and his passion for correct English style at one and the same time – 'the clever fooling of Touchstone and Audrey "brought down the house" more than once'. Not 'brought the house down' but 'brought down house'. How many journalists today have the same sensitivity to prepositions?

So much for the *hors d'oeuvres* – the 'informal luncheon' – and the *entrée* – the feast of culture. Now came the main course – the prize-giving and the speeches, which might prove just a little more indigestible.

But no. The report of the Headmaster, Revd E.C. Harries, was punctuated at frequent intervals by 'applause' and by 'hear hear', and ended to 'loud applause'.

Before that, of course, the School had to witness the arrival of the fossilised remains of superannuated gargoyles that are taken out of the mothballs to be paraded at every speech day and prize day – and have been so paraded from about the sixteenth century onwards. It's a wonder they're not wearing doublet and hose. It's another wonder some of them can make it up on to the platform.

In this case, the chief fossil was the Earl Fortescue, Lord Lieutenant of the County of Devon. So – a fossil of some power and eminence. Then came a delightful choice of verb – 'his lordship was supported' by . . . followed by the usual list. But 'supported'. Nice.

Once again, one is struck by the number of dignitaries that a small country boarding school could muster for its Prize Day – a mayor, four priests, five Justices of the Peace, and the aforesaid Earl. (As early as 1863, when the School was barely five years old, they had had the Archbishop of Canterbury.) The Headmaster also read out grovelling letters of apology from a Bishop and a Canon. Perhaps the priests turned up for the free lunch from force of habit. The Bishop and the Canon could do better in Exeter.

Incidentally, or rather coincidentally, also mentioned in despatches as 'supporting' his lordship was 'R.P. Chope', who had performed in a previous Shakespearian epic at the School as far back as 1881. This was *The Merchant of Venice*, and, since the magazine report said that *As You Like It* was the first public presentation of a school play 'for a good many years', it is likely that the *Merchant* was the previous Shakespearian epic. Mr Chope had taken the part of Shylock, and had only recently presented to the School a photograph of the cast in action in the 'pound of flesh' scene. That picture also survives, also in surprisingly good condition.

And so to the Headmaster's report. Like all headmasters' reports since the dawn of time, it ran the gamut of breast-beating, chest-puffing, and back-slapping, with perhaps the occasional side-swiping. Revd Harries wisely played his losing tricks first. There had not been many distinctions during the year. But before anyone could cry 'Shame!', he speedily weighed in with two fine achievements by G.E.L. Carter at Oxford, and an honours degree at Cambridge for John Britton. (Applause.)

Getting into his stride, and skating with cavalier dash over what might have been a lot of thin ice, Revd Harries informed the audience that 'everything had gone smoothly through the term'. I wonder what an audience might think if a headmaster today came out with such a sentence.

Perhaps they did frown a little in 1908, but Harries shrewdly did not give them time to let scepticism seep in. There was now heating in the east wing, the standard of work had greatly improved since last year, the standard of Maths 'in some cases promised to be brilliant', the cricket eleven was better than it had been last year, they had a new portrait of the late Earl to hang on their walls, and 'two fine silver cups' had been presented for cricket and football. ('Hear hear.')

Then it was sideswipe time. Any dictator will tell you that one infallible way of diverting criticism in a population is to have a war. A headmaster's version of this tactic is to launch a broadside against the educational authorities. Harries did the same – a brief but devastating salvo: he declared that 'the affairs of the Board of Education were in such an impossible condition that he thought the less he said on that

subject the better'. (No laughter. No applause. No 'hear hear'. They didn't know what to make of that one.) It was a brilliant coup. A damning indictment with no evidence needed. He let it be assumed that the audience understood the whole issue, knowing that nobody was going to interrupt the proceedings by putting up a hand and asking what the hell he was talking about. It was a perfect illustration of the 'emperor's-new-clothes' technique. And he was away to a new topic before anyone dreamt of confessing ignorance.

But he got through to them when he began to talk about secondary education. They applauded twice. They applauded again when he announced that only that day he had received permission from the Governors to apply to the War Office for leave to enrol a half-company of cadets.

One has only to read reports such as this, in fact any headline in any newspaper of the time, to become aware of a level of self-conscious national pride that, if carelessly expressed today, could land the speaker in front of a tribunal. But 1908 was in the middle of the flood tide of the British Empire. What else would a School jubilee celebrate but pride in one's country and in its unique achievement in putting together the greatest empire the world had ever seen, and in spreading the benefits of Christian charity and parliamentary democracy? What else could a School aspire to but to encourage boys to share this pride and to direct their steps towards taking their part in these worthy occupations and activities? They could not have done otherwise.

Look at the reports and articles. Look at the minutes of the School Debating Society. Look at the new cadet force. Listen to the songs of the music halls. Just because the sentiments expressed then seem today to be jingoistic, unfair, patronising, racist, and ignorant, it does not mean that they were not genuine and sincere, or that they were narrow and unkindly intended. Not only that; millions of young men were prepared, six years later to enlist, fight, and die for them. The School alone lost 56 of them, out of an annual roll of barely 130. Two of the prizewinners about to be rewarded by his lordship were to be wounded twice. Three died.

So Harries, in the following year, set up his Officer Training Corps, and willingly – nay, proudly – doffed his dog collar and put on his Sam Browne, and saw no incongruity and no irony in the change of wardrobe.

And if pride in one's country was certain to strike a chord of sympathy and understanding, the emphasis on a sound Christian education was to strike an even stronger one. Harries wisely left that to last, knowing that he was on the safest ground of all. He could assure Revd Thompson, the first Headmaster, and, now seventy-one years old, still a regular attender at School functions, that 'he need have no apprehension on the subject of religious education at that

School....While he had the honour of holding the reins as Headmaster, it would be his proudest privilege to see that every boy had a thoroughly sound religious education'. And more in the same vein. It received two 'hear hears' and two 'loud applauses'.

Time and again, one is left shaking one's head at the passion and certainty these men seemed to have. One may not necessarily agree with them today, but one envies their confidence and pride.

The prizes were distributed by Earl Fortescue. Some of the titles will occasion little surprise. The two youngest winners received, respectively, a copy of *The Jungle Book* and *Tom Brown's Schooldays*. There were two books from the Classics – *Stories from Homer* and *Stories from Virgil*. Again, nothing to wonder at. Only three books of a religious flavour though, and one of the recipients, E.H. Southcomb (whose family were to donate a shield to the School to mark the champion house), got his for Science. The two books on natural history were awarded to clever pupils in Maths. Oddly, there were five history books given out, though no actual History prize. Not so oddly, there were three books that celebrated empire. There was a prize for General Knowledge – *Shakespeare's Plays* – which should have taught C. Lewis a lesson. There were four winners of Science prizes, but only one of them received a book on a scientific subject.

As is often the case, some clever boys received more than one prize. W.L. Armstrong got four. In fact, although 21 prizes were given out, there were only 16 actual recipients – and five of those were members of the cast of *As You Like It*. Which reflects the old truism that to them that hath it shall be given. Or, to put it another way, however cleverly you devise a school system to reward as many pupils as possible, there will always be those gifted few who seem to mop up everything.

However, in fairness to today's system, (and after allowing for increased numbers), it is worth pointing out that, whereas in 1908 there were 21 prizes awarded, in 1999 there were 140. And a further 142 were mentioned on the programme. Of course, if the School in 1908 were only a seventh of the present one in numbers, the parallel is exact, and there is no point to be made.

Lord Fortescue then sang for his supper, or rather his luncheon, by making what the *Journal* called 'a most interesting speech'. Well, we weren't there, so it would be unfair to doubt this verdict. But his lordship went on for four pages, and the 'hear hear's' were pretty widely spaced out. However, they did appreciate his remarks about the objects of the School, and they clapped loudly when he said, with pardonable pride, that 'the founders can claim that they have been largely successful in putting the advantages of public school life within the reach of the sons of parents of moderate means'. (It is pointless to claim that he said nothing about parents of slender means. It was a major triumph that the founders had gone beyond parents of ample means; that was a first, and one has to start somewhere. The Government itself had only that year begun to pay out Old Age Pensions.)

There was a good deal of talk about playing the game, and being sportsmanlike, and putting one's team before oneself, and about learning to take pride in one's school, and telling the truth, and love of one's country, and defence of the Empire. It is easy to denigrate these sentiments too, because they have been so cheapened, hackneyed, and satirised since, and so often. But a cliché was a great truth once, and it was not noblemen who were applauding the Earl's remarks.

It was, as the Earl well knew, farmers and their families, for whom the School motto 'Read and Reap' was specially chosen.

However much we may be tempted to disagree with these men and their sentiments, even to laugh at them, the fact remains that they clearly thought that Britain ('Britain', note, not England) was best, that their School was a good school, that they subscribed to worthwhile ideals, and that these ideals were worth making sacrifices for. They would have left the premises – in their varied means of transport – feeling better than when they came. And they would face the years leading to the next jubilee with firm hope and confidence.

Old Boys' Day, 1908 – the Golden Jubilee Year.

Harries, Revd in the dog collar, and barely a a year into the job, is still looking very new, almost super-numerary. Thompson is in the middle, for once without his monocle. Between them is M.B. Snell, who had organised the Old Boys' syndicate to rescue the School shortly before, and whose name is over the door of the Library he founded. Third from left, seated, is Comer Clarke, whose wife wanted her money back from the Chapel Fund in 1947. Standing behind Clarke, with the twisted smile, is William Giffard, a young master, who later won the O.B.E. and the Greek M.C. in the Great War.

Despite the presentation of *The Merchant of Venice* in 1881, there does not seem to have grown any Shakespearean tradition at W.B. Harries tried to put this right in the year of the Golden Jubilee, with a production of 'scenes from' *As You Like It* , in the School grounds, to coincide with Prizegiving.

Statement of Receipts and Expenditure for Year ending December 31st, 1908.

Expenditure.

		£ s. d.	£ s. d.	£ s. d
To Tuition :	Salaries		852 4 4	
	Advertisements		75 5 3	
	Chemicals		23 2 5	
	Prizes		8 16 9	
	Stationery		17 2 4	976 11 1
„ Board :	General		4 5 6	
	Bread, Cake and Flour... ...		114 13 8	
	Meat and Fish		412 1 3	
	Dairy		95 10 4	
	Groceries		114 18 6	
	Vegetables		51 11 7	
	Ale and Mineral Waters ...		14 15 2	
	Coal and Coke		140 5 11	
	Oil, Lamps, etc.		40 9 0	
	Wages		373 3 9	
			1361 14 8	
	Less Masters' Board charged in Tuition ...	125 0 0		
	Balance of Garden & Poultry Accounts	44 8 4		
	Extras charged to Boys, etc. ...	97 6 3		
			266 14 7	
				1095 0 1
„	Rent, Rates, Taxes, Insurances, etc. ...		71 17 7	
„	House Repairs and Renewals		39 1 5	
„	Furniture Repairs & Household Requisites		45 9 7	
„	Mortgage Interest		57 0 0	
„	Improvements—Heating, etc.		81 11 8	
„	Sundries—Scholarships	58 16 0		
	Hire of Pianos, Chairs, Room, etc.	6 18 6		
	Secretary's Salary	25 0 0		
	Auditor's Fee	5 0 0		
	Inspection of Premises ...	1 11 6		
	Various	71 2 6		
			168 8 6	
				463 8 9
„ Law Charges	... ...			150 0 0
„ Balance to Profit and Loss	... ...			50 0 0
				£2734 19 11

Receipts.

	£ s. d.	£ s. d.
By Fees (Boarding, Tuition and Music)		1985 6 3
„ Devon County Council, Science Grant	148 6 8	
Scholarships	122 2 0	270 8 8
„ Government Grants 1907 (Balance)	122 10 0	
1908	314 0 0	436 10 0
„ Interest on £1,000 River Plate 4½ per cent. Debentures		42 15 0
		£2734 19 11

A School Accounts Statement for 1908. Look at the combined teachers' 'salaries'. If you think that is low, look at the combined domestic staff 'wages'. The total fees for the whole year would not pay for a single pupil's fees for one term today.

School Servants in the very early years of the twentieth century.

A view of the west approach to the School, in the days when the shrubbery and the unmetalled drive gave it a distinctly 'stately home' look.

A view of the School without the tennis courts – probably before the First World War. It is numbered on the back in the impeccable handwriting of Mr. A. Taylor, who taught here for thirty-four years and was also Secretary to the Governors. Note the ivy.

A view of the Karslake Hall, taken for a prospectus. Note that the ivy has gone.

A School photograph from 1911, just before the War. On the left of H.M. Harries, with the high collar, is Cecil Fry, who was appointed to teach Science; on Harries' right is Adelbert Taylor, who served the School in a host of capacities from 1895 to his death in 1929. He was known as 'Judy' Taylor because he had a voice like Mr Punch.

When Mr Knight was Headmaster, between 1900 and 1907, some pupils clearly thought that his rule was a bleak one; they christened the School 'The City of Dreadful Knight'.

According to the report of the School Inspectors in 1905, the Headmaster spent, each week, in teaching, twenty-seven hours. The Inspectors did think this was a little excessive, because it was too much 'to allow him to keep so careful a supervision over the work of his assistants as would be desirable, and without which [he] will not be able to ensure that satisfactory methods of teaching and a high standard of work are maintained throughout the school'.

HARRY, ENGLAND AND ST GEORGE – AND THE DRAGON

If a school is one hundred and forty-two years old, it would hardly seem surprising that it can boast a clutch of ex-pupils who have represented their country in sport. West Buckland is no exception to this law of chronological averages. Whether it measures up the national norm in the matter of actual numbers is another matter. I have no means of knowing. I should think it highly doubtful whether any researcher has felt it worthwhile to compile a survey of independent schools – with tables to compare their age, numbers, resources, grounds, facilities, opportunities, and parental and magisterial interest – which would enable him to draw up a series of national norms. A school has x pupils, has been in existence for y years, has z resources; its numbers are d, its facilities are tr x mp, and its parental and magisterial interest and initiative amount to bc x lsd over nbg. So it should have produced pi x ghq internationals – QED.

Well, who are ours?

Most people's memories are pretty short, so top of the list would come the most recent – a brace of beefy young men who became bastions of the England rugby scrum in the 1990s. One of them is now the proprietor of a chain of eating-houses. (Which leads to the speculation that someone could try and find out whether, or to what extent, an ex-pupil's international status influenced his later non-athletic career. A good subject for a Communications Studies project?)

The School has been playing rugby since 1925, so the cynic might argue that it was about time. But we have the answer for him there: there have been earlier internationals than Steve Ojomoh and Victor Ubogu. One old boy – Harry Packer – played for Wales in the 1890s, and another – Herbert Jones – played for England in 1950. Jones' rugby shirt now resides on the wall in the dining hall - moth-proofed (I hope) behind glass between the silver display case and the wooden boards recording the past presidents of the Old Boys' Association. So there!

And, if the cynic refuses to concede defeat, we could, if pushed, inundate him with a tidal wave of names of university and county players.

Returning to the fray, our aforesaid cynic might observe, that, while the School's rugby reputation is vindicated, it seems odd that, for a school that boasts the longest compulsory cross-country run in England, and going back to 1859, there have been no England marathon runners owing their start to the 'Exmoor'. No Olympic middle-distance runners either, come to that.

There, we must concede, he has a point. Some have come near – county and West of England and National Championships and so on, but none, to my knowledge, full internationals.

Yet, ironically again, our real world-beater, our Olympic Gold Medallist, our international and Commonwealth and World Games representative – our world record-holder, no less – is an athlete. Jonathan Edwards has beaten the lot, jumped (or rather hopped, stepped, and jumped) further than anyone else on the face of the planet. Of course his records will be beaten; any athlete's records will be beaten. That is in the nature of things. But, in his time, and on his day, Edwards J. (West Buckland and England) was without peer, and that is very satisfying for all concerned.

Edwards' real triumphs came after he had left school. Harold Gimblett's began while he was still a schoolboy. He was selected for the School First Cricket XI at an absurdly young age, and went on to carve a reputation that has dwarfed that of every other cricketer in the School's colours, and moreover dwarfed that of most of his fellow-Somerset players as well.

Nobody could have had a more story-book debut for his county. At Frome, on a Saturday in May 1935, barely out of school, he scored 123 in eighty minutes, without giving a single chance. His first 50 came in twenty-eight minutes, and his century in only sixty-three. He hit three sixes and seventeen fours. Within a year he was playing for England, though his career, like that of so many other great cricketers, was interrupted by the War. It must be said that his record in the England cap was neither long nor record-breaking, but he was one of the most exciting players ever to be seen with a cricket bat in his hands. For nineteen years, in 329 appearances for his county, he electrified grounds, galvanised crowds, and reduced bowling attacks to rubble. It was the sheer speed with which he did it.

Nor was he any crude rustic slogger from the deeps of the West Country. He was an opening batsman, for Heaven's sake. Anyone who scored as fast as he did, as regularly as he did, and as much as he did (including a memorable triple-century), had to be a stroke-player with a sound defensive technique too. I had to do a spot of research for these paragraphs, and I particularly relished one anecdote I unearthed from a history of Lord's Cricket Ground, by Sir Pelham Warner. During the War – 12 June 1943, to be precise – there was a match between the Army and the Civil

Defence at Lord's. Over 500 runs were scored in a day's play, and Gimblett's contribution was 124 in one hundred minutes, during the course of which he hooked a hapless bowler called Nichols full pitch right into the middle of the Mound Stand – a carry of 130 yards.

In a discussion of the varying talents and achievements of these gifted sportsmen, it may cross the mind to wonder whether they have any qualities in common. What have you got to have before you get selected to play or run or jump for your country? And what does your school give you towards those mysterious ingredients for internationalism?

Again, our friend the cynic might observe that if you can stand up to the conditions at West Buckland in winter you can stand up to anything; but that would argue for a far greater number of internationals than we actually have. It is not sheer size or strength, because another of those internationals is not only a fencer, but female – our only one so far. She is, or was, Charlotte Read (now Brown), and she was captain of the Women's Sabre Team in the recent Commonwealth Games in Kuala Lumpur. Gold medallist too.

It is unlikely to be raw talent, because so much time, money and preparation – in a word, professionalism – goes into sport at the highest level that raw talent will not get you far. Or if it does, and even if it gets you to the top, it is unlikely to keep you there.

I am reminded of a remark made by one of the judges in an international piano competition. The finalists were displaying their prodigious talents before the audience, and, during the interval, this judge was asked to summarise what he was looking for in the winner. He said that it certainly was not pure talent; it was assumed that no finalist would be there if he or she did not possess that in abundance. Nor was it dexterity, or a phenomenal technique. Nor was it the good fortune, or the low cunning, to give the compulsory concerto an interpretation that was favoured by the panel of judges. Nor, even, was it necessarily the ability to bring the audience leaping to its feet in a roar of wild adulation.

'No,' he said. 'What we must ask ourselves is whether this or that young pianist has the ability to sustain a whole career at the keyboard.'

So it isn't naked talent, or skill, or cleverness, or fiendish preparation, or whatever; it is some other quality which enables the exponent not only to become the best, but to remain the best – at Grieg's Piano Concerto or the sabre or opening the innings or propping up the scrum or whatever. This of course only answers one question by posing another, and the discussion could go on.

Which leads me to a further speculation: supposing all these gifted sportsmen were able to meet, would they find it easy to talk to each other in spite of their diverse activities? And in spite of the great age span

between some of them. Our earliest internationals achieved their triumphs a century before the last.

My belief is that they would find plenty to talk about. Imagine a group of engineers meeting across the centuries. I don't think the ancients would quail in disbelief and terror before today's modern wonders; I think they would be fascinated. Put a Roman aqueduct-builder and a medieval siege expert and a Baroque architect in front of the Millennium Dome, and they would at once be crawling all over it. (Again, our resident cynic would say that this would come after they had unanimously laughed or turned up their noses.)

So too would our internationals ignore each other's fashions and modes of speech, and would at once be deep in the mysteries and martyrdoms of their calling: the enormous pressures resulting from carrying the weight of the compliment – the compliment of representing one's country; the worries and self-doubts; the carpings of the armchair experts and critics who are so quick to discern early signs of waning powers – or what they claim are waning powers. They would share the double curse – the elation and the fear of being at the top, whence there is only one way to go, and that is down.

Messrs Ojomoh, Ubogu, Packer, Jones, Edwards, Gimblett and Ms. Read would find their conclusions endorsed by Harold Hilton, the golf international who won the Amateur Championship four times and the Open Competition twice, in 1892 and 1897.

Hilton has left us a written record of what it takes to make a good golfer, though I doubt whether he seriously intended all of it to be studiously followed by his successors. He described the day he first handled a club, at the age of eight:

'I essayed forth with one of my father's clubs, and I am told that I also annexed one of my father's hats, and as his measurement of head is nearer number 8 than 7, the sight must have been somewhat ludicrous. But in those days I didn't care much what clothes I wore. . . .

'I first held the club low down, with the shaft standing out past my left ear. I drew the club back in quite an easy fashion; but the downward swing was different, as just as I should have reached the ball the handle of the club came back and hit me on the cheek, and, I am told, "the hat came off". It has come off many a time since. I then decided to try with the handle on the other side of my head. In consequence there was mischief to be found on the upward swing, as once again did the handle strike me, but this time it was on the right cheek. I came to the conclusion that there was another method to employ, and that was to hold the club at the end. I found it more successful, as I avoided injuring my own person; but at the same time, I managed to strike another small boy on the side of the head, and thus ended my first attempt at the game.'

Thank God he got better. Though, like Frank Sinatra, he did it his way. A sports writer later described him thus in the Open Championship of 1901: 'He nibbled at big chunks of chocolate, and, of course, the inevitable cigarette never went out, for as soon as one died another revived from the ashes.' Enough to give a modern coach heart-failure, as well as himself.

The entry in the School magazine that carried these titbits was chock full of references to other Old Boys who had distinguished themselves in sport. To be honest, there was only one more full international mentioned, but the pages swarm with names that were obviously names to conjure with in 1907. The full international was actually a master, T.H. Judson, who had played rugby for Wales. But H.G. Bryant, W.H. Culverwell and E.E. Hammett had played for Somerset, and Searle for Devon. J.H. Potbury had represented Devon and the Western Counties at shooting, and won the all-comers' prize at Bisley. F.W. Grenfell had won the gold medal as amateur swimming champion of Scotland. The Revd E.C. Harries (yes, *the* Harries), it may not be generally known, had played cricket for Somerset, and J.R. Barber, an ex-captain of the First XI, played for Middlesex. (This man, Barber, has a distinction that is not strictly relevant, but which cries out to be recorded: he became captain of a cricket team called the Crouch End Vampires.)

Footballers were well represented. Another assistant master, C.A. Pauls, had played for Preston North End. The book says 'the famous Preston North End team'. Whether it meant that all Preston teams were famous, or whether it referred to the unique team ('Proud Preston') that went through the League one year without losing a match, and went right through the F.A. Cup without conceding a goal – alas! we do not know. T.H. Watts not only played football for Notts County; he played cricket for Devon, and held the School record for throwing the cricket ball – 105yds and 3 ins (which would take a bit of beating today).

And so on, and so on. Pick up any School magazine of the last fifty years, and one could probably find similar entries. M.E. Hodge and G.F. Bayles played for England Schoolboys. Bayles was later selected to join the Barbarians tour as the obligatory non-capped player who is always included in the team. Non-capped maybe – but the Barbarians! Take the recent decade: David Pote, who was reserve in the England Under-19 Rifle Team – when he was only sixteen; Tim Alldis, who has played cricket and been on foreign tours with junior England teams.

How many of them, and others, will join that select band of Gimblett's and Ojomoh's and Hilton's? How many future ex-pupils will prove to be true mavericks and – like Hilton – carve international reputations in sports which they were not taught to play at school?

In these days of accessible world-wide travel, years out, foreign university grants, and the global village, will we one day be recording in the School magazine the first international cap at volleyball – for Cambodia? Will some enterprising graduate transplant the game of hockey to Costa Rica, and become the captain of its first Olympic team? Will we boast our first ice-dancer, from Sri Lanka? Our first, what you might call, 'cerebral' international at, say, chess or bridge? Our first bobsleigh team (who had their early lessons pushing the cricket roller)? Our first Wimbledon Men's Tennis Champion – my word, that'll be the day.

You may think it fanciful to compare the modest tennis potential among our ex-pupils with the genius of Fred Perry, but funnier things have happened. In the late 1890s, the Headmaster was a Mr J.B. Challen, who, among other things, was a Welsh international footballer and a Somerset cricketer. He ran a Masters' XI while he was here, and he must have revolutionised North Devon. He was twice involved in one-day games which saw 500 runs scored in a day's cricket, and there was another two-day game which saw over 800 runs scored. I should guess that there are few clubs in the area which can call up memories like this from their records.

Challen's own figures for that side are truly remarkable. In 1896 he scored four centuries, with an aggregate of 988. In 1897 he scored only two, but was in the seventies and eighties twice, and twice made 97. In 1898, he scored seven centuries, and notched up an aggregate of 1285 runs, in only 15 innings. That same year, the Great Man, the Champion, Dr W.G. Grace himself, needed 41 innings to accumulate 1513 runs – only 228 more. Challen's batting average for 1898 was just over 85, which was more than double that of Grace. And Grace, at fifty, was far from fading; he had ten more years of first-class cricket left in him.

So a young headmaster in an obscure West-Country school could eclipse the Champion. And it is no great debating point to claim that Challen had it easy with feeble opposition; you should see the scores recorded by both sides. And remember both Challen and Grace had some fiendish wickets to bat on. None of your modern shirt-fronts.

So – if Challen and Hilton and Read could do it, who knows? Maybe we are already nurturing another Fred Perry, or a Stirling Moss, or a Stanley Matthews. But they will have their work cut out.

A youthful, and very purposeful, Victor Ubogu – rugby international. Here he seems to have discovered a secret hidden from the members of the scrum. He now runs a chain of food bars.

Steve Ojomoh, rugby international, next to a victorious junior sevens' captain.

Harold Gimblett, Somerset and England, with an appreciative first eleven.

A very slight Jonathan Edwards, on the left of the front row, before he broke the world triple jump record. Standing in the middle row, fourth from right, is Victor Ubogu.

Charlotte Read, fencer for England and Great Britain, and gold medallist at the Commonwealth Games.

W.E.L. Wall ('Eustace') winning the long jump, an event which he made uniquely his own, winning it three times, 1922-24. In 1924, he jumped an incredible 22ft 1in. For over twenty years, no West Buckland athlete came within two feet of it.

The early balance sheets of the School's accounts are set out in a manner opposite to that of professional practice today. I showed one, just out of interest, to Rosalie Priscott – resident guru in the Bursar's Office, piano teacher, Justice of the Peace, walking encyclopaedia on matters financial, and daughter of the village.

'Ah,' she said, 'they had Expenditure on the left and Receipts on the right. Nowadays, it's the other way round.'

Now – when and why did the reversal occur?

Cheap at the Price

In the balance sheet of the School's accounts for the year ending 31 December 1908, the total income from all fees, from all pupils, for the entire academic year, was £1985.6s.3d.

This sum would not pay the fees for one pupil for one term now.

How To Be A Successful Officer

Not long ago I came across a War Office letter dated March 1909, which in effect authorised the setting up of a cadet force at West Buckland School. By coincidence, I found this letter during the month of March, so I was able to announce that the School's Cadet Force – now renamed the C.C.F., because it incorporates the other two arms of the services as well – was exactly ninety years old. A fine, boastworthy military tradition was now safely documented.

I also found a photograph of a cadet camp at Aldershot, dated 1910, with a group of shirt-sleeved, hobnailed cadets who, so the caption claimed, came from West Buckland School. Fine. Most commendable. A credit to their generation.

A casual dip into the Minutes of the School's Debating Society would reinforce this attitude of unthinking loyalty to King and Country – an attitude which would be so nobly and tragically reflected in the devotion to duty and sacrifice that were in such evidence during the First World War. A school with about 130 on its average annual roll gave over 50 lives of its boys, staff and servants.

All the more surprising, therefore, to come across a small book in amongst all the photographs which poked fun of the entire system. You expect criticism, satire and plain rudery in the first decade of the twenty-first century. We are shocked by nothing; we are taught by our present education system to question everything; rules are there only to be challenged; we are let into all secrets by our television screens, so that we know everything and are in awe of nothing. We speak with the arrogance and confidence that come from cosy homes, full stomachs, and the latest technology. But this book – *The Young Officer's Guide to Knowledge* – came out (or at least its fifth edition did, which is the one I have) in 1917. ('Fifth Edition – Revised and Enlarged.') At the height of the 'King and Country' philosophy, when Kipling was gospel, and duty and obedience were Holy Writ. At the very worst time of the Great War – the War to End Wars. When there was nothing to laugh at about the mud of Passchendaele. And the fact that it was the fifth edition is an indication of its popularity. It's a wonder that the Army did not suppress it.

Why? Take a look at the very first page – the one about 'Maxims'.

Maxim Number 1. 'Never do other people's work, unless you are driven to it. If you do, you will get an evil reputation for liking it.'

Maxim Number 2. 'Always ask for leave at all times and in all places. In the end, you will acquire a kind of right to it.'

Or Maxim Number 3. 'Remember that there is a time to work and a time to play. The time to work is when you are being watched.'

Well, you may say – nothing very mutinous about that. Just a wry joke or two about Service life. Or any other kind of life, come to think of it. True – but what about Maxim Number 4?

'Abandon every vestige of individuality. In the Service it is considered indecent, and verges on insubordination. Most young officers join with a distressing amount of "originality", and it is only on reaching the status of Member of the Army Council that an officer can be said to be completely purged of it.'

Surely this would have caused some moustaches to bristle and gold braid to curdle in the Imperial General Staff? Particularly as the author was an Army officer himself – Captain C.G. Nassie Blomfield. With a name like that, you would automatically have placed him on the side of the Establishment. Unless the very name was itself a spoof. Unlikely, because there is a photograph of the man, and his regiment is identified – the Royal Warwickshire Regiment – which is, or was, genuine.

Why was he not court-martialled? Such mutinous, snook-cocking in time of war? As Captain Manwaring would have unhesitatingly said in *Dad's Army*, 'We'll have none of that sort of talk.'

But they did. And much more.

On generals: 'Whatever the General's fad is, study it well. It may be boots, it may be barrack-room shelves, it may be potato-peeling, or it may be an unsavoury delight in examining bare feet. The General may be a Tooth Brush Maniac or a Refuse Heap Wizard. In any case, always anticipate him.'

The Quartermaster 'presides over the rites and mysteries of this hallowed place [his stores]. The Quartermaster is never wrong. If you should be so unwise as to dispute any question with the Quartermaster. . . the Quartermaster will convict you out of the sacred books of the law, the Clothing Regulations or the Equipment Regulations.'

Or again, a laser-like observation: 'Adjectives are never placed in the right order in the Quartermaster's Stores. It is part of the abracadabra of the Quartermaster's Stores. One fine summer's day becomes "Day, summer's, fine, 1".'

If you are ill? 'Before being admitted to the Military Hospital you have to go sick. You must go sick at a certain specified hour. This does not necessarily mean that you must be sick. But you must go officially sick at a certain time, generally about 9 a.m., no matter what time you really began to feel sick or ill.'

Then two acerbic comments on phrases beloved of the military.

'Without Fail.' 'This expression is in constant use in the Service. It implies a premonition on the part of the user of the expression that there will be failure.'

And 'Reasons in Writing'. 'Generally speaking, an officer is only asked for his reasons in writing when it is well known that he has none to give.'

And so on and so on. One acid drop after another. Again, one wonders why the writer was allowed to get away with it, especially in time of war. Well, you may say, did not the rank and file sing rude words to popular tunes – about bad generals and stupid orders and gigantic military cock-ups? Yes, they did. But it is impossible to nail down the transitory treason of

beery sing-song in an estaminet in Picardy on a Saturday night. It would have been a simple matter to arrest the proclaimed author of this little hard-back, the more so as he was an officer and a gentleman.

Apparently, nobody did. Or if they did, they did not prevent his seditious little volume running into at least five editions. It would be interesting to trace the publishers – 'Harrison & Sons of 45, Pall Mall, S.W.', or their successors – and ask if there were any further editions, and how the book came to be printed in the first place.

The publishers themselves gleefully climbed into the joke, by quoting in the front 'Unsolicited Testimonials'. They claimed that the *Military Review* [if it existed] said it was 'packed with the concentrated essence of military wisdom'.

And the 'Adjutant' was quoted as saying, enigmatically, 'The C.O. wishes to see you at the Orderly Room immediately'.

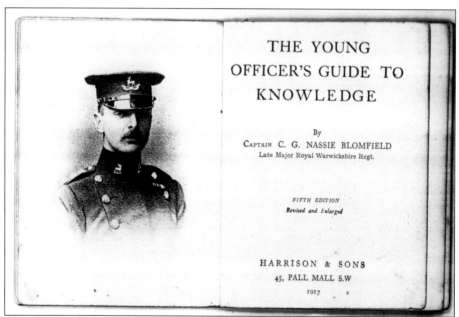

The frontispiece and author of a highly scurrilous book about the Army, published, incredibly, at the height, or rather in the depths, of the First World War.

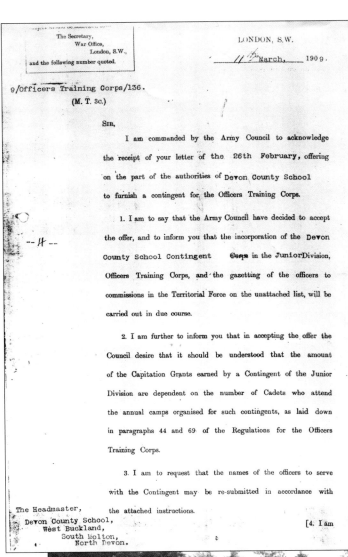

The letter from the War Office authorising the Headmaster, the Revd Harries, to set up a cadet force, known then as an 'Officer Training Corps'.

The first-ever Cadet Force, or Officer Training Corps, July, 1909. The Revd Harries has eagerly exchanged his dog-collar for a Sam Browne.

The O.T.C. at Aldershot in 1910. The tents look like a gathering of the Ku Klux Klan.

The Officer Training Corps in 1913. Even before the outbreak of war, it represented about forty per cent of the School.

An early cadet camp, at Farnborough, probably before the First World War. With the blankets and bush hats, they look like swagmen about to blend into the outback.

A recruiting drive by the Devon Regiment in Ilfracombe, 1915. The O.T.C. are at the rear. The boyish writing on the back of this card says, 'A little way down you will recognise Mr Harries. Behind him are our school corps. I am marked with a (X).'

The Officer Training Corps in 1918 – officers and N.C.Os. The number of officers has grown to three – a reflection of wartime pressures.

A School shooting team, 1919. If the Great War had not ended, who knows how many of these boys would have been called up – and killed. Look at their faces.

A School shooting team from 1938, with similar faces. How many of them, one wonders, survived the *Second* War?

The full corps of drums, with some splendid equipment. Date about late 1930s, from the officer's style of uniform, and from the format of the picture's mounting. There are a lot in this style from the 1930s.

A corps of drums on the march four or five decades later. It looks like H.M. Michael Downward and Housemaster David Clark towards the back. With the high hedgebanks, it provides an odd mixture of the military and the rustic.

A cadet camp which seems a long way from the Farnborough 'outback' expedition of the early years. This lot look more like Yugoslav partisans loaded down with demolition equipment to make life difficult for the Nazis – Force 10 from Navarone.

Another group from a cadet camp of 1964–1964 BC, ancient British commandos in a coracle.

A Family Tragedy

Mr Tom Miller, of West Buckland, had three sons, who all attended West Buckland School: William (1893-1895), Frederick Thomas (1904-1906), and Reginald John (1908).

In April 1917, Reginald was killed in action. Later in the year, William died at West Buckland. On the very day of William's funeral, word arrived that the third son, Frederick, had been killed in Palestine. Mr Miller had lost all three sons in nine months.

In the summer of 1917, the Headmaster attended a course at Gosport on physical training and bayonet fighting, and obtained a satisfactory certificate (*Register* No. 164, Dec., 1917, p294).

Answering the Call

Mr Watson, the music master, who had come to the Staff in 1897, joined the Armed Forces in 1918 – at the age of forty-five. The *Register* reported him as 'struggling with the theory of gunnery at Portsmouth, and spending his spare time in tackling the clarinet'. It concluded, 'May a speedy peace soon restore him to the orchestral rehearsals, and may he bring his clarinet with him.'

It did. The *Register* of March 1919 joyfully applauded his return. Whether he brought his clarinet with him is not recorded, but the likelihood is that he did, because he, and his piano, (and his clarinet?) became the musical mainstay of nearly twenty years of Gilbert and Sullivan productions after the War. He was on the Staff for over forty years – possibly the longest-serving teacher of them all.

[The episode is eloquent evidence of the immensely powerful pull of the War upon able-bodied men at home – the insupportable spur to the pride. Anything was better than being left behind – trench slaughter or no trench slaughter. This feeling was clearly not confined to young bloods of nineteen or twenty. It reached out to a middle-aged music teacher in the deepest recesses of North Devon.]

Grenville House was born in 1918 (*Register* No. 167, Nov., 1918, p. 69).

❁ REMEMBRANCE DAY ❁

1998 marked the eightieth anniversary of the Armistice signed on 11 November 1918. The eightieth. The number of people still alive who remember it is small. The number of people who were fighting in the war it brought to an end is still smaller. The men who fought in the Second World War are seventy or more; the men who fought in the First must be about a hundred.

What significance can all that possibly have for a young person today? Put like that, not much. What meaning can a Remembrance ceremony hold for him, or for her? Again, not much. A person in middle age would have had a father or grandfather who took part, but a child now would not even have that. Grandfathers alive today would be too young to have joined the Colours in 1914. Most would not even have been born.

Leaving aside the debate as to whether the ceremony should be continued, and accepting that we do have a ceremony this year, how can one treat it so as to offer any significance to a young audience?

One way may be to try and bring home to them what that war, what any war, means to those who took part, and to those who saw members of their family go – and in many cases never return.

The writer R.F. Delderfield, who attended West Buckland School in the mid-nineteen-twenties, wrote some reminiscences of his time there. The first public ceremony he had to attend as a boy was the Remembrance service on Armistice Day in 1926. Only eight years after the end of the First World War. A war which took altogether nearly nine million servicemen's lives on both sides, including 56 old members of West Buckland.

The School was gathered round the War Memorial outside the Hall. It was a parade; nobody asked the boys whether they wanted to be there. The Headmaster, the Revd Harries, was a figure of legendary authority, in a period when the stiff upper lip of the public school was universal. One did not question orders, and one did not show emotion, certainly not in public. Harries made a short speech about those 56, nearly all of whom he had taught as boys in the previous twenty years or so, nearly all of whom he had watched grow up and leave, eager to make their mark on the world.

When the speech was over, a bugler played the Last Post. The writer, Delderfield, says he happened to be standing quite close to Harries. As the notes of the bugle carried over their heads, he saw tears streaming down Harries' cheeks.

That incident was echoed in a paragraph about the Second World War that appeared fairly recently in the Sunday press.

In Normandy, there are, as is well known, tens of thousands of war graves, of men who died on D-Day in 1944 – the Normandy landings – or shortly afterwards. If you visit one of those war cemeteries, you may be surprised to discover that they are lovely places – quiet (obviously), but fondly tended, and most imaginatively and beautifully laid out. The sadness comes when you read the inscriptions on the gravestones – not the names, but the ages – 19, 18, 20, 17, 18, 17, 19 and so on.

The piece in the Sunday paper was by a journalist who had also visited one of these cemeteries. On one of the graves he noticed a letter wrapped in cellophane which had recently been left. The young man in the grave had been nineteen years old when he had been killed.

The letter was written in the spidery hand of a very old man. It was telling the young man in the grave the news of what had been happening in his family: 'Your sister Pauline died last spring. Your brother Derek is now living in Lancashire with his family. I have a new dog. . . . ' And so on. It was signed simply, 'Love, Dad.'

That letter had been written in 1996. The boy had died aged nineteen in 1944. Work it out for yourself. That man had been writing to his son for fifty-two years. He must have been over ninety. Whenever he had been able to make the journey, he had gone to Normandy and left a simple message of family gossip on his son's grave – the only way he could devise of communicating with the son he loved, whom he had lost so long before, and whom he had never forgotten. 'Love, Dad.'

Can young people feel what that old man felt? Of course not. Nor can they fully understand why Harries cried at the War Memorial. But many of them will become parents, or teachers, or both, one day. So they must be patient with the old men, even with the teachers. The time will come when they will understand. They will understand what oceanic depths of unspoken emotion can be summed up in a simple message – 'Love, Dad.'

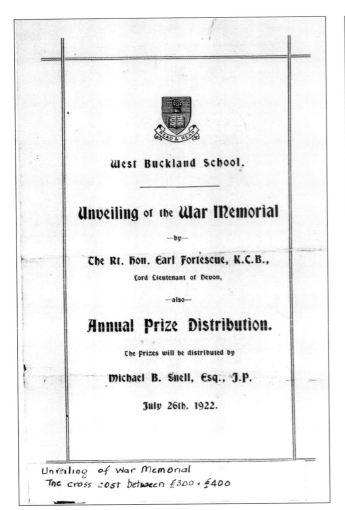

West Buckland School.

Unveiling of the War Memorial

—by—

The Rt. Hon. Earl Fortescue, K.C.B.,

Lord Lieutenant of Devon,

—also—

Annual Prize Distribution.

The Prizes will be distributed by

Michael B. Snell, Esq., J.P.

July 26th, 1922.

Unveiling of War Memorial
The cross cost between £300 + £400

Another stone structure, unveiled, unfailingly, by Earl Fortescue, (the fourth Earl this time), in 1922.

FOREWORD

IN issuing this Roll of Honour there are several points which require explanation. It will be noticed that not only the regiment, but also the rank of the individual has been omitted. During the War many changed from one regiment to another, and even went into a different branch of the Service. It was, therefore, difficult to decide whether to record the one in which anyone served first or last. The rank was left out for another reason which I hope will meet with the approval of all, and that is that from a school point of view each did his best to maintain the school's traditions, whether commissioned or not, and that, therefore, it was somewhat invidious to draw a distinction among those who, while at school at any rate, lived on equal terms.

The list is, I feel, inaccurate, and has possibly many omissions. The omissions are caused by the fact that the school records kept prior to 1900 are almost useless, and as the O.B.A. was not formed before that date, the tracing of people whose names are in the old address book was, of course, hopeless; hence one must suppose that many who were at school about 1890 served, but because their addresses were not known, could not be communicated with. Whether, however, a feeling of "esprit de corps" should have caused them to send in their records or not is a matter of opinion. I cannot accuse myself of any lack of effort, seeing that I sent circulars in all directions, and used the columns of the *Western Morning News*. I can only say now that if any serious error is discovered I will acknowledge it in the School Magazine, and see that the official copies of the Roll of Honour are duly amended. These copies will be filed at the School itself, and will be sent to the chief libraries in the county. Elsewhere a summary of the list will be found.

SUMMARY

TABLE A

	Number who Served.	Killed.	Died of Disease.	Wounded.	Mentioned in Despatches.	Distinction.	Commissioned.
OLD BOYS	357	44	9	62	21	32	140
MASTERS	8	1	0	1	1	2	7
SCHOOL SERVANTS	2	1	1	—	—	1	—
TOTAL	367	46	10	63	22	35	147

TABLE B

Members of the School O.T.C. Contingent, who are included in the above list.

Number who Served.	Killed.	Died of Disease.	Wounded.	Mentioned in Despatches.	Distinction.	Commissioned.
105	19	3	30	7	13	90

The O.T.C. Movement was started 1908 and the West Buckland School Contingent was formed in 1909.

Two pages from the Roll of Honour for the First World War. It was a generous and touching idea not to include rank. The final figure rose eventually to 56 – out of an average school roll in the war of less than 130. Though this proportion, incidentally, is by no means rare among contemporary schools – rather the opposite.

A School group from 1919, immediately after the Great War. Compare the formality and stiffness of this group with the lounging and posing of the 1884 group.

A School Second Eleven from 1914. The *Register* did not print the names of the team, but we know from one of the match reports that, in the match against Bideford G.S., on 6 June, 1914, 'Perry's innings of 57 was quite the outstanding feature of the game'. In the return match, on 4 July, his bowling was 'excellent'; he took 4 wickets for only 3 runs. And he 'made 34 not out in the second innings'. Against Wellington School, on 8 July, he took 4 for 18, and contributed to 'the fourth win for the Second XI'. They only played four games. We also know from the Roll of Honour that 'William Everard Henry Perry was killed on 1 April, 1917'.

The School First Eleven from 1914.
Thirteen boys altogether played for the School team that year – T.E. Hayward, the captain, A. Nevill, J.L. Carter, J.P. Stewart (or 'Stewart-Burton'), W.E. Berry, J.H. Berry, J.G. Mellish, C. Charsley, G.H.D. White, A.G. Lewis, C.B. Callender, K. Ogden, and H. Boutroy. Every single one joined the services, ten of them in 1914, probably in response to Kitchener's famous call that 'Your Country Needs YOU'. Callender won the M.C. Boutroy was wounded twice; Charsley four times. Carter, who also won the M.C., and was mentioned in despatches, died of disease. Mellish was killed in 1917. White was killed before 1914 was out – three days before Christmas.

A very young-looking Second Eleven from 1935. How many of them did not come back from the Second World War?

And the even younger Colts of 1935. What about them?

✖ A Typical Product ✖

I worked for a decade or so at a grammar school in Surrey. When the time came for the entrance examinations to be taken, the prefects saw to the business of welcoming parents and candidates, showing them to the right places, calming nerves, answering questions about the school, and generally cultivating good relations. Many potential parents told me that it was both interesting and informative to compare their ten- or eleven-year-old hopefuls with the eighteen-year-old veterans who were looking after them. To see, if you like, the material before it entered the process, and the finished product.

I work now at a public school in Devon, where substantially the same thing takes place, when senior pupils show potential parents round the campus. Either way, if parents wish to find out something about the work of the school they are interested in, the process gives them some means of doing so.

Of course, it helps them with their crystal-gazing only so far as eighteen. Where and how could they find out about the sort of mature adult the school produces, in the longest of long runs? Speech Day will regale them with an impressive array of university degrees and other honours won by former pupils, and occasionally – very occasionally – an old member of the school will become famous. But it would be unfair to judge the general run of ex-pupils by the rare exceptions who attain celebrity. And it could also be argued that graduates might not be the norm of school-leavers. A fair percentage leave at sixteen, for instance, and another sprinkling go into the services or family businesses.

So – assuming first of all that the question can even be fairly put – what, in that longest of long runs, would be a typical product of the School?

It is not simply a matter of asking a cross-section of old boys and girls what they think, because their answers will be coloured by reminiscence – whether good or bad. I have noticed that recollections of West Buckland seem to be firmly favourable or unfavourable. They either loved it or they hated it. Virtues and sins are trotted out with equal willingness.

For example, W.B. is strong on sport; it encourages a lot of other outdoor activities; there has long been a powerful cadet tradition; the boarding element has a great binding influence on its inmates; there is a strong family feeling among all who live and work there – pupils and staff alike.

On the other hand, it is often accused of being far too devoted to sport, at the expense of other activities;

those who excel at sport have often been too much lionised; more recently, the accusation has been levelled that the needs of girls have not been sufficiently addressed; for many years the boarding facilities were, to say the least, a mite spartan; for an equally long time, the School was not noted for its academic strength, though there were many powerful individual performances; its very remoteness gave it a sort of time-warp dimension, as if it were a couple of decades behind the rest of the country. And so on and so on.

Even within families, opinions could be, and were, divided. One brother would love it; another would hate it. Few old members (I nearly said 'survivors') seem to dismiss it with a noncommittal shrug.

So – how do we find out? What would be, as I said, the typical product'?

Can we get away from extremes – away from glittering successes among former pupils, away from pouting rebels, away from sullen drop-outs? After all, by definition, the average pupil would not be any of these extremes, and he would be in the majority.

Not long ago, I could have come across him. (I say 'him', because he was at the School long before co-education struck. I intend no slur on girls. It is simply a fact that, of the fourteen decades that the School has existed, twelve of them have been as a single-sex establishment, so, if a 'typical' WB pupil exists, he is likely to be male.)

Let us call him Ted Woodman (and I offer up a silent prayer that there has never been an old pupil called 'Ted Woodman').

Ted Woodman was born in 1911, came to the School in 1924, left in 1928, and died, full of years, only a few weeks ago, aged eighty-eight. He got his School Certificate (the equivalent of G.C.S.E.'s today), served in the Cadet Force, performed in the inter-house Glee competition, picked up two or three academic prizes, and did quite a lot of cross-country running. Which is hardly surprising in a school which prided itself on its military and cross-country traditions.

He left to join the Merchant Navy, but, when the Second World War broke out, joined the Army. He served right through till 1945, rose to the rank of Major, and fought from the D-Day landings right up to Arnhem and beyond. From start to finish he remained with the Devonshire Regiment. He was proud of his regiment, and later did valuable research work in the regimental archives.

When peace came, like many ex-servicemen, he wondered what he could do, after six years of training which had fitted him only for war. He bought a small business, and over the years developed it into a successful enterprise involving machinery.

He took part in local life; he became a magistrate, a town councillor, a local school governor, an endowment trustee, a tax commissioner, a local historian, a church charity fund chairman. He married and had four children. He stayed in Devon.

Many testimonies were recorded both during his life and shortly after he died – about his conscientiousness, his fair-mindedness and commercial probity, his leadership and care of his men in wartime, his Christian citizenship, his charity – for instance in employing, immediately after the War, a German ex-prisoner of war. And so on.

Dedication, fairness, probity, leadership, Christian charity – most schools would be content with a testimonial like that for their pupils.

Of course, West Buckland cannot take all the credit. That would show stupidity as well as unseemly vanity.

But it is worth noting that Ted Woodman, commended by his peers as well as his subordinates for his kindness, sense of honour, and Christian virtues, was at the School under the headship of the Revd Ernest Harries – and the two facts cannot be entirely unconnected. Again, Ted had a rich vocabulary, and it is hardly coincidence that he was almost certainly taught by one of the School's great English teachers, Sam Howells. (And, incidentally, Ted picked up two English prizes during his time.) His love of History would appear to indicate that he came under the influence of a gifted teacher in that subject too somewhere along the line; most young people catch the history bug when they are at school. And he surely owes some at least of his ability to survive six years of war, hardship and discomfort to his four years of cold dormitories, freezing wash basins, and mud-soaked, smoky-breath, heart-pounding cross-country runs.

No doubt he became what he was because of a lot of other factors too – the War, his marriage and family, his business, to say nothing of his own innate virtues. Any person becomes what they become through a welding of factors during their lives. If you like, a sort of fusion of elements – if such a chemical process is possible. So the School can take some credit for providing one at least of those elements.

Whether Ted Woodman liked the School or not is immaterial; it helped to make him, and at a very impressionable time in his life. I don't suppose he liked the War much, but that helped to make him too.

If any school can have a hand in turning a boy into such a Christian character, such a many-sided human being, such a well-loved husband and father, such a valuable member of the society in which he lived, that is a monument in which it can take legitimate pride. It might easily settle for that as its typical product.

A smartly-coiffeured class from the days when P.E. was known as 'Drill', and the teacher as often as not was a 'Drill Instructor'.

The School First Eleven in 1920. Note the two types of cap. The 'skull-cap' type of headgear for colours, complete with tassel, was transplanted to the rugby team when the switch was made in the 1920s.

A comparatively rare photo of a Second Eleven, also from 1920. Second from the left at the back was Mallanah, one of three brothers (S.S., S.J., S.M. – known as Jimmie, Johnny and Jackie) who attended, and served the School well, between the Wars. S.J. became School Captain and won the Fortescue Medal, and his C.V. in the *Register* leavers list runs to thirteen lines.

The Common Room, from a prospectus of the inter-war period.

The Karslake Dining Hall, from an inter-war prospectus. One wonders whether the table linen, and the servers' ties, were put there just for the photograph.

The original Phoenix Society, 1926, which arose from the ashes of the old Reading and Debating Society, which had been founded in 1903. The complete Minutes of that early society are in the School Archive. Note that the Phoenix tie had already been designed.

A School photograph from 1921. The War had not killed the high Eton collar.

The oldest high-jump technique of all – from a School Athletics meeting in the 1920s.

Alan Barbary and J.A. Kerrich fighting it out to the tape in the 1920s. It looks like Harries doing the recording.

At what was probably the same meeting, F.G. Hill and Monty Bate are clearly some way from the tape, judging by the spectators' lack of interest.

That 1920s' meeting again. The purists would have something to say about the hurdling technique here.

A preoccupied Harries with devoted runner from another 1920s' meeting.
Look at the remarkable near-perfect mirror-image of the other two teachers
at the high jump.

In 1920, the Revd E.C. Harries, Headmaster, was elected President of the South Molton Football club (*Register* No. 173, Nov., 1920, p. 255).

The Flaming Fairy

One old member of the School remembered being a fairy in a school play – and a very resourceful one too. When, during a performance, his costume caught fire, he tried to save himself by wrapping himself in the front curtain. In his urgency, he overbalanced, and fell out of the wings on to the keys of the piano. 'Up dashed. . . the French master, who lifted me up, put his arms round me, kissed me on both cheeks, said "Oh Pouf" and extinguished the flames.'

▣ LITTLE HELLERS ▣

Tom Hitchins came to West Buckland School in 1928. Many of his memories of it, over seventy years later, are as fresh as if he had left yesterday.

Nor has his life been exactly uneventful since he left in 1933. He is understandably proud of many of his achievements. The list on offer here is incomplete because he was answering an Archivist's questions, and he modestly stuck to the point. But, for instance, he was a very early Territorial officer, well before Hitler began to threaten the peace of Europe. He served in the Artillery right through the Second World War, and was a survivor of the military misadventure in Norway in 1940 ('a botch-up'). The flotilla which evacuated him and his tired comrades was only a short distance behind the ill-fated *Glorious* ('another great cock-up'). He served in the T.A. for years after the War too.

He played rugby till he was fifty-eight ('only the second fifteen, you understand'). [Only!] He has served as President of the O.W.B.A. and as Governor. He is a member of the W.B. Masonic Lodge. Both his son and his grandson attended the School, and both became Head Boy.

He has served on countless committees, councils, panels, and boards connected with the School. He has attended every Old Members' dinner in Plymouth since he set up the first one in 1933 – except one ('gammy knee – all right now'). And he has missed very few in London too.

He comes from a Plymouth family, and his elder brother had preceded him to W.B. by a year or two. 'Hated the place.' Tom clearly did not; affection, loyalty, and pride shone through everything he said about it.

Tom had been sent to the School simply because his brother had been. He met six boys on the platform at Plymouth Station – Peter Matthews, three brothers Warne ('S.E., J.D. and P.E.' – father was a printer from St Austell), C. Turner and A.S. Groves. Together they rode to Exeter, changed for Dulverton, and then changed again for Filleigh. Then, carrying their overnight bags, they walked all the way from Filleigh Station to the School (Tom admitted that their heavy luggage was brought up later by lorry).

If the walk from Filleigh to W.B. was a stern test for a new boy, it was a fair preparation for what was to come. The School may not have been exactly the Colditz that some more selective memorialists would have us believe, but it was not a holiday camp either. Tom was fair and balanced in his assessment.

Yes, you did occasionally have to break the ice on the water in the washbasins [what negligent matron had allowed old water to stand there long enough for ice to form?] but on the other hand, when you came back from a run, you could 'usually get a spot of hot water'. No, the food was not as good as it is now, but it was 'adequate; I never starved'. True, no dormitory window was allowed to be completely closed – day or night, summer or winter – but there were 'very few in sick bay'. Tom claimed that the first time he slept in sick bay was when he was an Old Boy and came back for a visit.

There was no central heating in dormitories, but there was in classrooms – till the boiler broke down. Tom remembered classes huddled in cadet greatcoats. But people seemed to survive; Tom has no memory of any epidemics during his time. [Perhaps the germs couldn't stand the open windows.]

The great advocate of this healthy, Spartan living was the Headmaster – the Revd E.C. Harries – 'Ernie'. He was Headmaster for twenty-seven years all told, and had been at the School as a junior master a few years before that. His influence was everywhere. He was clearly a latter example of what was once known as 'muscular Christianity'. Ernie believed in discipline, fresh air, exercise and the value of sport. He was reputed to go for a daily early-morning run – in shorts. He exercised his dog 'Bob' himself – no deputing the chore to some hapless, chilled junior with blue knees and sleepy dust still in his eyes. He coached rugby, and joined in, and expected the boys to tackle him – and he did this right into his sixties.

With such a champion of sport at the top of the School for so long, it is small wonder that rugby and cricket and running and swimming played such a large part in the life of the School. Nor is it a surprise that the skilled exponents of these sports were lionised. Tom's brother was not much good at sport, and didn't like the School; Tom was good at sport, and loved it.

It was sport which underpinned the ancient custom of fagging at the School, which, it may surprise some to read, was still going on in the 1920s. (And, I gather, continued, in one vestigial form or another, right into the 1960s.) To come out in favour of fagging these days is like saying that you approve of foot-binding in women, or that you would bring back public hangings.

Tom nevertheless would not condemn it outright. 'No – it taught boys to respect seniors.' Did it not encourage bullying? 'No. Your senior – you usually fagged for only one bloke – saw to it that you were not put upon by others. Seniors were anxious to ensure that your treatment by them was not seen as bullying.' What did you have to do as a fag? You looked after the sports kit of a games Colour. This could extend to taking the laces out of his boots and scrubbing them white. Surely small boys hated this? 'No. You took pride in how your bloke was turned out.' Moreover, seniors offered rewards 'most times – chocolate – things like that'.

Who was allowed to have fags? 'Sixth-Formers and School Colours' [the sports thing again]. Tom did not go into the debate as to whether it was worse for the character of the fag or of the fag's senior, but then he wasn't asked. And he remained plain and honest about it. 'I don't think it was a bad thing. Perhaps I was lucky.' And he went on to become a Colour, so he too had a fag – as he freely admitted.

The modern world must beware of becoming too hypnotised by features of bygone days which have become unfashionable, even reprehensible. Conditioned by modern democracy and correct politics, they are taught to regard things like fagging, caning, skivvying, waiting at table, and so on, as demeaning and dehumanising, and eagerly interrogate survivors of it as if to try and elicit ghastly horror stories and scandals – so that they can thereby justify the attitudes they themselves have acquired. The survivors, on the other hand, who never thought much about it at the time, find it difficult to see what all the fuss was about.

One thing Tom was prepared to concede: the School is now a more comfortable place than it used to be. Which is hardly surprising. A simple list of 'modern' aids to human ease would readily prove that – full central heating, tuck shops, sixth-form bars, snooker tables, covered swimming pools, gas rings, telephones – fixed and mobile – to say nothing of all the electronic gadgetry to enhance personal entertainment. Any honest modern reader of this could no doubt add another dozen.

But perhaps it made the denizens of the 1920s a trifle more creative. 'After Church on Sundays, you could go to the local farm and buy currant buns from Mrs Stanbury. If you ordered in advance, you could have custard tarts.' With a weekly allowance of sixpence (two and a half pence), you would have to be creative.

Boys didn't get out much, but games players of course had away matches. 'Before you came back, you would stuff two bottles of scrumpy into your games holdall' for later, more furtive consumption. Another expedient for the outdoor types was to obtain a piece of solid fuel and an empty receptacle like a salmon tin, with a pat of butter or fat, repair to a convenient thicket in the grounds, light the fuel under the tin, and cook an egg or two – 'pheasants' eggs very often'. [I bet Delia Smith doesn't know about that one – nor Keith Floyd – not even the Naked Chef. More

likely to be familiar to those old members of the School who joined the S.A.S.]

All this makes one wonder whether they found time to have lessons. But – yes – they did. Harries again was to the fore; he taught Latin. Was he a good teacher? 'Yes,' said Tom simply. Was he ever afraid of him? 'No. I had a very great respect for him. But I wasn't afraid – no.' Tom did concede that he had a healthy wariness of a certain P.E. teacher.

His most influential teacher was S.E. Howells – 'Sam'. Sam made you mind too. To such an extent that if the preceding lesson had been taken by a lax disciplinarian, the moment the poor wretch had walked out of the room, it would fall silent, because they were expecting Sam any minute. Like many successful teachers, Sam had a peculiarity, which, in a lesser man, would have made him a figure of fun; in his case, he couldn't say his r's. A regular term of abuse was to address the whole form as 'you wetched little spawwows'. And not a smile would appear.

But Sam encouraged good work. He kept a book for it. If you did a praiseworthy piece, you were encouraged to write it up in the book, and you got half a crown for your trouble. True, he could be sarcastic ('he could make you feel that high'). Now if there's one thing boys don't like it is sarcasm, but even there Tom was fair – 'I don't think he ever over-used it.'

Finally, Sam bore two of the hallmarks of the good teacher. He was enthusiastic, and he was memorable. 'Sam taught me poems I can rattle off now that I haven't seen in print since I was here.'

With the emphasis, necessarily, on the Spartan life, and the all-pervading influence of sport, it is difficult to see the West Buckland of Tom's time as a mecca for culture. But Sam Howells' spell had clearly done its work on outdoor boys. And there were two other features of School life which must be mentioned.

The Glee has only recently disappeared. Tom didn't have much to say about the Glee, except to chuckle and say that his house, the Grenville, was usually last. 'We were the "rogue" house.'

The other facet – one might almost say 'phenomenon' – was Gilbert and Sullivan opera. Every year for years the School mounted a full opera – *Iolanthe*, *The Yeomen of the Guard*, *The Pirates of Penzance*, *The Gondoliers*, *The Mikado*, *H.M.S. Pinafore*. The appearance of ladies among the teaching staff after the First World War no doubt helped in casting. One or two old boys came back to sing principal parts. The music master, Mr Watson, played an awful lot of piano. But when all was said and done, it remains an amazing achievement for a small boys' school of about 150 to 180 to put on a production like this. A glance at the surviving photographs shows, for example, what enormous trouble was taken with the costumes.

Such a tremendous effort requires an inspiration, a drive. And guess whose that was? Right first time – the Revd E.C. Harries. Ernie adored G. and S. He usually played the principal part (and even if you regard the whole thing as a huge ego trip, the fact remains that it needed a huge fund of enthusiasm and energy for a busy teacher and Headmaster to learn and rehearse and lead in the way he obviously did). Tom's matter-of-fact verdict on the operas was that they were 'pretty good'. Sadly, they did not survive Harries' retirement.

In between inspiring the operas, and teaching Latin, and taking his dog for walks, and running the School, Harries was also an officer in the cadet force, or the Officer Training Corps, as it was then. In the Archive is the original letter from the War Office authorising Harries to set up the Corps – in 1909. Innumerable photographs survive of groups, and bandsmen, and camps, and corps of drums. Tom played the bugle, and later gravitated to the cymbals. [An odd progression?] He obtained his Cert. A, and attended two cadet camps at Tidworth. Apparently, the cadets were an option in those days – which is a surprise. From all that one reads and hears, one would have thought that in that more regimented atmosphere, it would have been compulsory. Was this a sign of Harries' enlightenment, or evidence that the School could not afford enough uniforms?

The teacher who ran the cadets was a Mr Corless – Captain J.E. Corless – 'Jasper'. Other members of the staff rated random remarks from Tom's memory. Like 'taught French – very dark – excitable' or 'inoffensive – pleasant – retiring - bachelor, I think'. Or again 'taught games – hefty – nice feller'.

When it came to his contemporaries, Tom's memory was displayed in richest detail. He could not only call up scores of names; he supplied initials as well. Lots of intriguing hints – 'growing oranges in South Africa last I heard of him' – 'day boy, had a foot amputated, rode a bike to school, had a tin fixed on the pedal and stuck his stump in it' – 'did well in the Indian Civil Service, a delegate at the Partition negotiations' – 'ran flat-footed, you'd think he wasn't moving, but he was'.

There was a chilling piece of evidence of how cruel boys could be to a weak disciplinarian. Tom and his mates had a man for chemistry who was 'clever, but useless as a teacher'. Before the lesson, they emptied the contents of a jar of sulphuric acid and replaced it with water. At a prearranged signal, one of their number, right under the teacher's nose, drank the entire jarful. The poor man was beside himself.

No doubt the culprits received six of the best – from Ernie, of course. One detail stands out for sheer oddity. Those sentenced to receive such punishment had to attend Harries' study, at lunchtime, in their pyjamas. Apparently this was to ensure that no books could be shoved down trousers to lessen the impact. An educational reformer today would have a fit.

Tom harboured no grudge about it. He pointed out that Harries was not a frequent beater, and usually did it only in order to bolster the discipline of weak staff. Tom remembered a time when, after Harries had beaten him, he took Tom for a walk in the grounds and proceeded to have a friendly conversation with him.

Always we came back to Harries. Any man who is Headmaster for twenty-seven years must leave some kind of a mark. But with Harries it clearly went deeper than that. When he took over, the School had been through one of those rough times which are going to afflict any school with a long history. Harries pulled it round. 'He saved it, and he made it,' said Tom. His wife was also well remembered.

Another odd detail. Harries' mother, after she was widowed, came to live in the School. Tom cannot remember much about her, but she must have been some kind of a force, because a full portrait of her appeared in the *Register*. There can not be many schools whose official magazine carried, as a frontispiece, a photograph of the headmaster's mother.

Tom's reminiscences left the listener with a very coherent impression of this small, remote school in the back of beyond, which nevertheless was able to create a great sense of purpose and of belonging – at least in those who found its ethos congenial. No doubt there were misfits, as there would be in any school, and their 'misfitting' is not necessarily their own fault.

And Tom was in no doubt as to who was responsible for its success. 'Harries held the School together.' 'He was a great man, and a very human man.' This bustling, busy, interested, confident clergyman, with his endless energy, and 'one little hair on his nose bobbling in the breeze'.

Curiously, it was Harries in a way who provoked Tom's only criticism. Harries had three sons, all of whom attended the School. Tom provided details of their later careers, then paused and mused for a moment.

'Little hellers when they were here. . . and you couldn't touch 'em!'

ERNEST CHARLES HARRIES
HEADMASTER AND CHAPLAIN OF
WEST BUCKLAND SCHOOL 1907-1934,
BORN 7TH JUNE 1868 — DIED 10TH MAY 1954.

SIS MIHI, CHRISTE, COMES.

ALSO ELEANOR HIS WIFE
BORN 27TH MAY 1886 - DIED 7TH DEC. 1985.

Ernie Harries' grave in East Buckland Church. His wife lived to be nearly a hundred.

WEST BUCKLAND SCHOOL FIRE

Destruction of Prefects' Studies and Library

On Saturday night a fire occurred at West Buckland School, near Southmolton, where there were 160 boarders. Fortunately there were no serious consequences except damage to property.

The secretary to the school, Mr. E. E. Hodge, left the main building at about 10.30 p.m., when everything appeared to be in order. At ten minutes to 11 Mrs. Harries, the wife of the headmaster, detected a smell of smoke. She reported it to the senior house master, who ran to the first floor in the head prefect's study. On his opening a door a big volume of flame shot through the corridor and blazed up in the prefect's study. Luckily the portion alight was situated at the eastern end of the block, and therefore away from the students' sleeping quarters. The buildings involved comprised a large schoolroom, two classrooms, and the physics laboratory. A chemical laboratory adjoined.

When an alarm was raised the scholars were mustered and formed into a chain to provide a supply of water. The boys worked splendidly. The effort to confine the fire to the point of the outbreak was successful.

Southmolton Fire Brigade, under Captain J. H. Buried, quickly responded to a call, and water was playing on the flames within a few minutes of their arrival. At first water was derived from a large well, which held out for half an hour or more. Then the engine was taken to the cricket field, where water was taken from a swimming bath.

The damage included the destruction of four prefect's studies and the general school library. The more valuable reference library was saved. In order to save the physics and chemical laboratories the fire brigade had to put up a big fight. Except for damage done by water, their labour in this connection was successful. It is understood that the loss is covered by insurance.

Another account says: The fire was discovered partially through the uneasiness of a dog belonging to Mrs. Harries, and the promptitude with which the outbreak was dealt with was due to the fact that many of the staff and prefects were up later than usual on Saturday night owing to listening to the broadcast of "The Yeomen of the Guard." The school has an operatic society, which annually performs one of the Gilbert and Sullivan operas, and consequently more than usual interest was being taken in the Saturday night broadcast.

At 10.30 p.m. the building was quite in order. The secretary of the school, Mr. Eastmond E. Hodge, stated that at that time he went around the premises. Some time between 10.45 and 11 p.m. Mrs. Harries noticed that her dog was restless and behaving strangely, and she then detected a smell of burning.

She immediately notified the senior resident master, Mr. S. E. Howells, the headmaster being away in London. Mr. Howells had himself noticed a slight smell of burning, which was traced to the eastern wing to the playing-fields, which is entirely separate from the general dormitories and other school premises. In this wing are four prefects' studies on the first floor, and on Mr. Howells opening the door flames belched out across the corridor, and drove back the master and the prefects who were with him.

The whole of the studies were then involved in flames, which had got a good hold. Immediately on Mr. Howells making the discovery the whole of the 150 scholars and household staff were round, and a messenger was sent to the village post office, nearly a mile distant, to telephone for the Southmolton Fire Brigade. The brigade were called at 11.10, and were on the scene with their motor fire engine within 20 minutes, together with Police-Sergt. Venton, of Southmolton, and Constables Abrahams and Chilcott. There was not the slightest panic among the boys. They behaved admirably throughout. With chemical extinguishers and

The press report of the fire at West Buckland School in March, 1930.

The 'Great Fire of 1930', which attacked the Chemistry rooms, the Phoenix Room (and burnt a book of Minutes), and Prefects' Studies.

Views of the damage.

The morning after the fire. Prefects here are l. to r. W.G. Turpitt, D.W. Lister, A.L.J. Davies, G.C.J. Pearce, G.F.J. Thomas, and the Revd Watson, Chaplain (the third member of the staff by that name).

This stone was laid just over seventy years after the third Lord Fortescue laid the first.

Building the Memorial Hall.

The opening of the Memorial Hall by the Bishop of Crediton, 12 October 1932, nearly two years after the famous fire.

Inside the Memorial Hall.

The Memorial Hall, shorn of its crowds, scaffoldings, and opening trimmings.

One Man And His Dog

In 1937, the ex-Headmaster, the Revd E.C. Harries, was compelled to put his dog, Bob, to sleep. He had clearly been a School character; few School photographs in those days were complete without him. It was Bob's persistent barking which had led to the discovery of the famous fire in 1930.

Another Glimmer of Equality

Although the School can be fairly said to have 'gone co-ed.' at the end of the 1970s, it had girl pupils before that. The record must go to Vivyan Lindsay and Jane Horne, who attended West Buckland in the 1930s. They were the daughters of Mr Westall, the Headmaster from 1934 to 1939. They were invited as guests of honour to a recent O.W.B.A. dinner.

THE SAFE UNDER THE LAVATORY BASIN

One of the great might-have-beens of West Buckland's history is the School Chapel.

In the Archive is a small collection of yellowing letters, together with two bunches of much-folded semi-transparent sheets of paper held together by ancient brass split pins. They chart the progress of the scheme to provide the School with a chapel. The correspondence is incomplete, and the surviving drawings are tantalisingly short of a full picture. Nevertheless, one can put together enough of a narrative to give an impression of what could have been a worthy addition to the School – to its general appearance, to its dignity, to its spiritual life, and to its general atmosphere and *ambiance*.

The correspondence begins with a letter dated 5 July, 1935, and addressed to the Headmaster, Commander R.V.N. Westall. If Commander Westall was the original mover in the business of a school chapel, this in itself produces an irony. The School had had three previous Headmasters in holy orders – Thompson, Watson and (recently and famously) Harries – but so far as is known to this writer, there had been no initiative towards such a building. Perhaps it was felt that the connection established very early with East Buckland Church was sufficient; perhaps the School's finances never showed enough surplus to offer the possibility of such a spiritual luxury; perhaps previous Headmasters had not had enough experience or knowhow in the matter of fund-raising. Whatever the reason, it was left to a layman, Westall, to start the ball rolling.

The writer of the letter, a Mr A.L. Tamkin, from Twickenham, enclosed a quick sketch of his first thoughts on the subject. He apologised for its having been done from memory – which indicates that he might have been an Old Boy. And since he included in his sketch the War Memorial (which was unveiled in 1922), he would appear to be a fairly recent Old Boy – or maybe a previous parent. At any rate, he had access to the library of the Royal Society of British Architects, which seems to show that he had either architectural qualifications or connections. He suggested a building at the corner of the Memorial Hall, facing the front drive past the War Memorial. Roughly where one of the hockey goals is today.

Taking 200 as his working figure for the proposed congregation, he offered it as his opinion that the Chapel could be built for £7000.

There was one odd thing about his sketch; he orientated the Chapel north and south rather than east and west. It looks from the drawing as if the altar will be in the south end. But, as he said, he was doing it from memory. His knowledge of the buildings may have been sound, but his navigation was somewhat on the blink.

However, the letter must have given the Headmaster and Governors enough encouragement to proceed, for the next letter comes from a firm of architects in Torquay, indicating the willingness of the senior partner – Mr G.S. Bridgman – to come and have a look 'without involving you in any liability'.

By the middle of September, Mr Bridgman was submitting preliminary sketches for the Headmaster's consideration. The general style of the proposed building was to be somewhere between Early English and Decorated – in proletarian English 'pointy arches and windows', with big square stones round the edges. So at least it was going to look like a church. None of your fancy Guildford or Liverpool modernism. Trust the Devonians to go for something traditional – in a county where Drake would not allow something so trivial as an armada to interfere with the important business of a local game, and where they hadn't heard of decimal currency till 1985. ('Daun't ee worry, mah dear – they waun't get they decimal coins down yer fer yurrs yet.')

Put Devonians up against Margaret Thatcher, and they will make her look like a Robespierrean revolutionary. The irony is that they still vote Liberal. Perhaps that is not so much a gesture towards modernism as a throwback to Gladstone and Lloyd George. If a candidate turns up one day with a name like Asquith, he'll romp home.

However, that is by the way.

There followed various letters about the position of the pews – facing inwards or facing forward – the siting of the organ, the question of the gallery, and so on. Mr Bridgman was not happy with the figures cited by the original Mr. Tamkin, who at some stage had also quoted, it appears, the sums of £5500 and £7500 as well as his original £7000. Mr. Bridgman is moved to observe, 'I cannot think where Mr Tamkin got his figure £5500', adding pointedly 'unless it was from a Nonconformist chapel which we have recently designed'. But this, he pointed out, 'was of brick and quite plain and only allowed chair seating and no tracery windows'. It is difficult to escape the feeling that the well-meaning Mr Tamkin had caused a bit of confusion.

The School had added to the confusion by altering its estimate of the number of seats it wanted, from 200 to 296, which would raise the cost to nearly £15,000.

Thirdly, the School chaplain, who had naturally been consulted, had put in his two pennyworth (or rather more), because Mr Bridgman also observes, 'Your Chaplain seems to have some rather strong opinions and in view of this I should like definite rulings on the following points.' And there are a lot. The School trimmed its sails, but Mr. Bridgman could not get the estimate down below £9500. This was confirmed by a letter from a Mr Hills, a Torquay surveyor.

At this point, a gap opens in the record, for two years. The next letter in the series is dated 4 May 1938, and is from Shapland and Petter, detailing proposals for panelling, seating and flooring. It would seem from the general context that the Governors were now discussing plans for an appeal to parents and Old Boys, and by June Mr. Bridgman was discussing his scale of fees (which included his pretty substantial travelling expenses from Torquay – 'at 3d a mile').

Further summer letters discussed things like the length of the pews, the Chaplain's room, the barrel ceiling, steel roof trusses, and the business of making the intervals between the windows the same as those between the existing ground-floor classrooms. The drawing also showed details like the stairs up to the gallery, the heating facilities, and the iron cover to the coal hole. There was reference to details of seating – 26 for staff, 236 for pupils, and 34 for the choir. (As with new school blazers, there seems to have been here a generous allowance for growth.)

Right out of the blue, though it had obviously been discussed before, comes this sentence: 'The small safe for communion plate can, I think, be placed under the lavatory basin.'

It is so incongruous, and so unexpected, and so *à propos* of nothing that had gone before, that it is difficult to think of any comment worthy of such an arrangement. As Eric Morecambe would have said, 'There's no answer to that.'

By this time, a fair momentum seems to have been generated. Stationers were writing with details about the format of the Appeal communications that were to go out to parents – and presumably to Old Boys as well. There was a Post Office form to be filled in about pre-paid reply cards. Mr Bridgman was already referring to that ingredient which always seems to seep into any building project, large or small – increasing costs: 'I know this figure is somewhat higher than you antici-pated'. The second inescapable factor of any building project also had to be addressed: the matter of planning permission.

In August, Southwood's ('Heraldic & Exclusive Stationers – 16 & 17 Burlington Arcade, W.1' – nothing but the best) submitted their invoice for 1700 sheets of 'Kings Windmill Vellum' and 1700 'Business Reply Folders', which, together with a few other bits and pieces, came to the sum of £22.13s. The School paid – in full – six weeks later.

In September, the South Molton Surveyor accepted the plans. By late autumn the money was coming in. Only four samples of this correspon-dence survive in this file, but there must have more than that, or the project would not have continued. By November, Mr Hills of Torquay was talking about floors and ceilings and plastering and heating and lighting.

Then, right at the end of December, Mr Bridgman was congratulating Mr Westall on his new appoint-ment to another school. Mr Bridgman assumed that the new incumbent would 'have much to occupy his time before he can give attention to this project', and realistically concluded that the whole scheme would probably lapse for about a year. There is no surviving letter to indicate that Mr Westall disagreed with this prognosis.

Mr Bridgman decided very prudently that the sooner, therefore, that he asked for his money, the better. Accordingly, taking time out from the New Year celebrations, he had prepared his invoice by the 3 January 1939. For work which had dribbled on for over six months, which had involved preparing rough plans and working drawings and scale drawings, obtaining estimates, and numerous discussions and visits from Torquay, to say nothing of preliminary calls and talks as early as 1935, he charged the total of £68.12s. He anticipated further charges as the work progressed later (he was being either correct here, or merely optimistic), and suggested a payment on account of £60.

By way of response to this, the School sent £40 'on account', as the scribble says on the architect's letter. Mr Bridgman's reply was not a happy one. The payment would, he said, barely cover 'out of pocket expenses'. He made a personal appeal to Mr Westall to do something about it.

There the correspondence ends.

And there does not seem to be much in the way of material to fill in the gaps, or provide the postscript. For instance, the relevant entries in the School magazine are sparse. In the number for July, 1935, the appointment is recorded of a new Chaplain, the Revd J.H.B. Andrews. He was the one who, according to Mr Bridgman, had the 'rather strong opinions' recorded above.

In the autumn of that year, there was, apparently, an 'epidemic in the neighbourhood', which had necessitated keeping the pupils away from East Buckland Church. (Not that that would have caused a great deal of spiritual anguish, one suspects, to the more philistine elements in the pupil body.) However, those charged with the religious education of the boys in their care may have wondered then whether the provision of a School chapel would get round this problem.

At any rate, the Headmaster, in his Speech Day Report a year or more later, in November 1936, made the following observation: 'By next September they hoped to be fully equipped in every way, except one; he looked forward to the day when they would have their own School Chapel.' There is no mention of how this item of news was received.

A year later, the Revd Andrews left, and was replaced by the Revd W.E. Wroughton. Had the departing Andrews had one or two too many 'strong opinions'? We don't know. We do know, however, that, besides outspoken, he was resilient; he later became Chairman of Governors.

Just as the correspondence falls silent in 1937, so, it appears, does Westall – part of the time. He makes no mention of a chapel in his Speech Day Report of November of that year. At any rate, no mention of a chapel is recorded. However, the Minutes of the Governors' meeting in the same month state that he 'outlined a scheme for the provision of a small School Chapel'. Note the word 'small'. He went so far as to specify '60 to 70'. Yet, in the correspondence with Mr Bridgman, a higher figure had been mentioned. Indeed, Mr Tamkin's original working figure of 200 had been raised to 296. To be fair, Westall did also say that the design would allow for possible extension at a later date, but 70 up to 296 does seem to be a large 'extension', and Westall was already catering for it in his early correspondence, and giving every impression that that was the original size he had in mind. Odd.

Even odder, at an Old Boys' meeting in the following March, Westall remarked that 'it was the policy of the Governing Body not to increase the size of the School as they believed it would alter its character'. He went so far as to say that 'if they had 250 or 300 boys the whole character would be altered, and he believed they would make a mistake if this were done'. So why plan for a chapel to accommodate a total of 296? Especially when Mr Bridgman was telling him that a chapel of the size he had requested would cost a lot more than they planned, or wanted, to pay.

Incidentally, when he did announce the Chapel scheme to the assembled Old Boys, it was received with cheers. At the next Old Boys' Gathering on Whit Sunday, his similar announcement was 'received with acclamation'.

Flushed with the success of this support, Westall, at the next Speech Day, in November 1938, announced formally that 'there would be an appeal to all friends of the School for funds to build a School Chapel'. Again, there was this curious emphasis on its small size – 'the Chapel, as they thought of it, would be fairly small, holding about sixty'. To be fair, he went on to stress that he did not intend to make any chapel attendance compulsory on any boy. But if that were the case, why, once again, make plans for a capacity of 270 boys and 26 staff? (The academic staff in 1937 and 1938 totalled 11.)

The same number of the School magazine (227) recorded subscriptions from Governors, Masters, Friends, Parents, Old Boys and 'Firms' totalling over £700. In a recent conversation I had with an old employee of the School, he told me that a sort of barometer had been installed in the School, recording the rising level of contribution.

Then Westall went – to his new post at Kelly College.

The new Headmaster, Mr Badger, made no mention of the Appeal at the Old Boys' Dinner, or at the Whitsun Gathering. In November 1939, no mention was recorded in the magazine report of Speech Day. The magazines of March and July 1940 said nothing about it. Speech Day came and went in November, and again nothing was said about it which the magazine thought worth recording. Nor did the Headmaster think fit to say anything about it in his report to the Old Boys.

The magazines of March and July 1941 said nothing. In November, not only was there no report at Speech Day; there was no Speech Day at all.

The trail had gone completely cold.

Not only was the trail cold; it had become muddied.

Skimming through a handwritten history of the School, in the Archive, I found a reference to a new chapel. An appeal, it said, had been sent out. This would tie in with the previous item recorded about Westall's announcement at Speech Day in November 1938. The puzzle comes with the amount. The handwritten history quotes, as the 'estimated cost', 'about £2000'. Beforehand, remember, there had been all this talk about £5000, £7000, £9500, and £15,000. This handwritten history, by the way, is (almost certainly in my opinion) in Westall's own writing. (The history is, incidentally, a fine tribute to his industry and persistence – to find time for this work in a very crowded Headmaster's day.)

It is possible, of course, that there was not one chapel scheme, but two. But if so, why did Westall keep one set of participants in the dark about the other?

Did Mr Bridgman ever get the rest of his money? Did the new Headmaster, Mr Badger, ever get around to giving his 'attention to the project'? What happened to the money that came in for the Appeal?

What killed it? The passing of Mr Westall? The

inability or the unwillingness of Mr Badger to attend to it? The inadequacy of the amount of money that came in? After all, £700 was not much against an estimate of over £9000. Or – most obviously – was it simply the War, which spelled the end of so many projects and good ideas up and down the country. Everybody had far too much to attend to.

I repeat, the record is tantalisingly inadequate.

One end was at last tied up. I had gone back to the Governors' Minutes. They were complete right up to January 1938, and I found another book covering the period after about mid-1946. The period in between – roughly the War years – remains a blank. I can find no record.

But – lo and behold! The second Governors' meeting recorded in the new book, in September 1946, comes up with this: 'On the motion of Capt. F.G. Glossop, it was decided that the Fund in existance [sic] for a Chapel be transferred to the School Account and spent on the Library, other cultural activities or any aid to worship.'

Interestingly, this Captain Glossop had been the Chairman of Governors who signed the Minutes of the very meeting when the Headmaster had 'outlined a scheme for the provision of small School Chapel' back in 1937. He had gone off to the War, and had returned only in 1946. The Minutes of the previous meeting, on 14 May 1946, had recorded the pleasure of his colleagues at his safe return from war service and at his rejoining their number. It seems likely, therefore, that Captain Glossop had been curious right through the War about all that Appeal money lying around in a bank account (hunched on the bridge of a storm-tossed destroyer in the North Atlantic, gazing into his hot cocoa, and musing, 'You know, Number One, I've often wondered what happened to that seven hundred quid, and if I ever get out of these hellish convoys, I shall make it my business to find out'), and one of his first acts on his return was to see to it.

Anyway, that is all I can discover. At least it was, until two recent coincidences. I came across two further, and separate, references to the Chapel Fund when I was looking for something completely different.

The first jumped out of the pages of the Governors' Minutes for 1947 – that trouble-strewn winter in which it never rained but it snowed, to coin a phrase. As if blizzards and blocked roads and burst pipes and scarlet fever and cancelling the 'Exmoor' were not enough, Mrs Comer Clarke, in the very depths of January, began asking awkward questions about the Chapel Fund. To put it more bluntly, she asked for her money back. One of the Governors, Miss Smyth-Richards, 'at the request of the meeting, undertook to explain personally to Mrs Clarke, the expenses that had been incurred, and to

ask that her claim might be waived'.

We presume she did, because there was no comeback from Mrs Clarke, or at least none that I have discovered. I must admit that I have not combed every meeting's minutes thereafter.

It seems a reasonable bet, does it not, that Mrs Clarke did not persist. But, amazingly, the Chapel Fund did. Again, quite by chance, I was thumbing through a book with the riveting title 'Financial Management, 1964-1982', and discovered several references to the 'Chapel Fund'. As late as 1969, it stood at £512.13s. – so it had dropped a bit from the original £700-odd. It appears that various payments had been made out of it in the intervening years, but it was still drawing interest. By 1971, it was worth £589.15.

Thereafter, several calls were made upon it, chiefly for a firm called the Compton Organ Co. Bits and pieces mostly. Something called 'Rotopress' accounted for another £59.48. Then, in 1976-77, a whopping £537.36 for 'Eustace and Alldridge', whoever they were. Interest was still dribbling in, but this declined, obviously, as the fund dwindled. On 1 April 1977, the Chapel Fund was recorded as being worth only £44.35, on which the interest was £2.22.

The following year, an entry on the balance sheet recorded that the Chapel Fund was 'closed'. But it had had a good innings, and it is quite easy to make a case that the calls made upon it in the intervening time fitted the criteria laid down by Captain Glossop's motion that the money should be spent on 'the Library, other cultural activities or any aid to worship'.

Natural curiosity, however, makes one wonder who 'Eustace and Alldridge' were, and what services they provided for their £537. I daresay there are plenty of people around with a long memory who could readily answer that question.

But I would bet that there are not all that many who could tell us whether the patient Mr Bridgman received his outstanding £28.12s.

So that was as close as the School came to getting its own place of worship. Probably its last chance too. In these days of community centres and ethnicity and multicultural religious education and counselling sessions and 'personal, social and moral education', it is difficult to see the money coming in for a traditional Church of England School Chapel with pointy arches and windows.

Even if it did, imagine the wrangling within the Chapel Design Committee. . . 'If we have a couple of confessionals for the Roman Catholics, we must have half a dozen counselling chambers to balance them.' 'This should be a building where pupils can commune with themselves; who says it should have anything to do with religion?' 'Well, I think there should be a quiet space somewhere – let's call it a

"Nirvana Corner".' 'Of course it looks like a Nissen Hut; we are designing a building for the twenty-first century, not a medieval chantry.' 'I still think it is a bad idea to have the safe under the lavatory basin; any decent "A" Level Maths candidate with alleged diarrhoea will have cracked that combination within a couple of hours.'

Ah, yes – another of the great might-have-beens.

But, if you can shut your eyes for a moment and picture a solid, new, school chapel, in traditional style, designed to fit in with the existing buildings – sizeable too, 92 feet long – at the angle of the Memorial Hall and the drive out towards East Buckland, it is a nice prospect. . . it would have looked good, wouldn't it?

A view of the School from the east, taken for a prospectus between 1922 and 1930. The War Memorial was unveiled in 1922 and the east wing was burned in the fire in 1930.

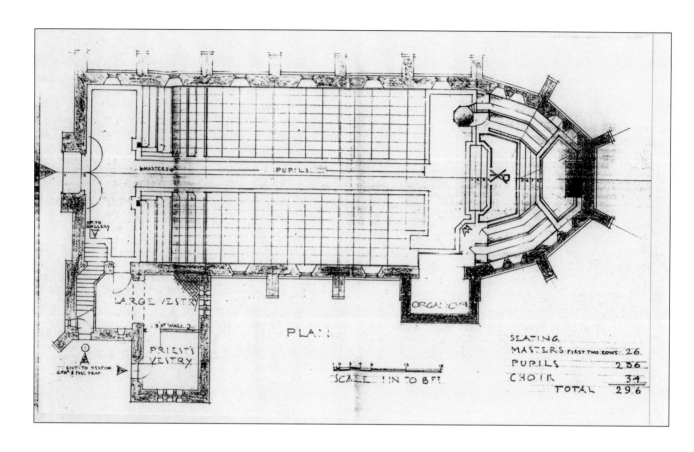

Two architect's sketches of the School Chapel that never was.

Views of the School. In many ways it looks, from the front, like everyone's dream of an old-fashioned Greyfriars-type of country boarding school.

This dormitory, while it is probably from a between-the-war prospectus, looks little different from the similar one taken before the First World War. Though they have changed the lampshades!

The gym. again, but the lesson is now probably called 'P.T.' instead of 'Drill'. The boys have advanced to the comfort of socks.

A summer afternoon in front of the School. With so many in white flannels, it could have been the day of the Old Boys' annual cricket match as well, at Whitsun. Notice all the tennis players got up in long trousers and turn-ups, like Fred Perry and Donald Budge.

The appearance of a tennis team only became possible with the construction of the new courts in the 1930s, by Headmaster Westall. Note the long trousers and turn-ups.

A post-war, more athletic-looking team, probably from the 1950s or 1960s.

Three of a Kind

In 1930, the Revd A. Watson joined the staff. Nothing remarkable in that – except that he was the third teacher called Watson employed by the School ('Register' No. 201). The first – another Revd Watson – was the Second Master under Thompson; he served as Acting Head when Thompson went off to study for his degree at Cambridge, between 1867 and 1871. The second – 'Watto' – was the longest-serving teacher the staff has ever had – forty-two years. He was the music teacher who played the piano – endlessly – for all the Gilbert and Sullivan productions between the wars.

There were three Daveys too. The first was Frank, who came in 1915 to teach French and Maths. He left – at twenty-four – to go to Sandhurst. The second was Cecil George, who served for four years, teaching P.E. – or 'P.T.', as it was then. He also left to join the Forces, in 1940. The third, and longest-serving by far, was Wilfrid Charles, who was educated at a little-known institution, the Barnstaple School of Art. He was the man who made all the long dining tables in the Hall.

In more recent times, the School has gone one better – with three more teachers of the same name – Clark (or Clarke) serving *at the same time*. To say nothing of yet another contemporary, Mrs Bunclark.

✖ Bodging On ✖

When Jim Hobbs was twenty, the Bursar at West Buckland School, Mr Hodge, asked him to come in to repair some glass breakages.

Why didn't he ask the resident repair man to do it? Because there wasn't one. The War was on. Supplies were short; money was short; everything was short. Two maintenance men had received their cards, because the School couldn't afford them. The previous Headmaster, apparently, had not been noted for his thrift – which hadn't helped – and, after he went, indeed throughout the War, everyone had to 'bodge on as best they could'. That was Jim's succinct summary, which could have been applied with equal aptness to a million situations up and down the country.

Why Jim? Because he lived in the village. He was convenient. He had the right sort of knowledge. He was, at the time, apprenticed to a firm of decorators in South Molton. So he came in to mend some windows.

He must have impressed Mr Hodge, because shortly afterwards Jim was offered a permanent post with the School, for £2.10s. a week (£2.50). Which wasn't much, even by the standards of the time. But this was Devon, and this was wartime, and this was a school strapped for cash.

Why then did Jim accept? Because it was better than a shilling a day (5p.), which was what he was getting as an apprentice decorator. In order to qualify even for that, he had to be at work in South Molton by seven in the morning, and the only way to get there was on a bike. Some days he had to work with his firm at Witheridge, which meant getting on his bike again. It made a round trip between West Buckland and Witheridge of 38 miles. So a half-mile walk to the School seemed a more attractive proposition.

It was no accident or coincidence that Mr Hodge had approached him. He was already known. His whole family was already known. Jim Hobbs is a classic example of a theme that has run through the history of the School like a vein of silver practically ever since its inception.

I refer to the Network. With two communities so self-sufficient and so remote from urban life and so close to each other as the School and the village, it would have been a miracle if their communal lives had not become so irreversibly intertwined. The School needed domestic labour; the families in West Buckland needed employment. It was a perfect marriage of convenience. This equation must have been particularly valid in the last quarter of the nineteenth century, when the School numbers rose to 150 at one stage, and when the Great Agricultural Depression struck, making farm work

difficult to find. It came to hit the School as well in the end, as farmers bracing themselves to tighten belts withdrew their sons from the vigorous young moorland academy outside the village.

But the bond between the School and West Buckland village survived, and in the twentieth century proved to be just as strong as before, and Jim's family is, as I said, a perfect example.

His father worked at the School for forty years, from the end of the First World War, mainly on the gardens. (The School had a long tradition of producing a lot of its own vegetables, so much so that this was frequently recorded in the School prospectuses.) His mother used to look after the children of one of the School's legendary teachers, Mr Taylor ('Judy' Taylor). Incidentally, Mrs Taylor taught in the village school, where Jim had been one of her pupils.

Jim met his future wife at the School, where she helped in the Headmaster's house, or 'the Private House', as it was known then. The Head at that time was Mr Badger, one of the two men who held office for only two and a half years between them at the start of the War. So Mr Badger, and Mr Smith, did not have time to make much of a mark. Interestingly, though, Jim remembered that Mr Badger and his family worshipped not at East Buckland Church, which was the official 'School' Church, but at West Buckland. That peculiar bond again.

Mrs Hobbs, as she was to become, also worked for the next Headmaster, Mr Howells. Both of Jim's sisters worked at the School at one time or another; one of them was nanny to the children of yet another Headmaster, Commander Westall.

Jim's brother was actually a pupil at the School, and later worked for it after he went into semi-retirement. It would seem that Jim had a choice about coming as a pupil himself, but he did not take to the idea. He reckoned that he was 'more reserved' and that he 'wouldn't have liked the life'. This could be the diplomatic criticism of the thoughtful and sensitive boy who decided that the spartan ethos and muscular, muck-in-together, ruggernaut heartiness of the Harries era was a mite too intrusive for his taste. I have come across this division of opinion between brothers before; one loved it and one didn't, each for the most genuine of reasons, and it is no reflection on any of the interested parties.

To bring this association right up to date, Jim's niece has also worked in the School, and is still there. Rosalie is the Presiding Genius, *Eminence Grise,* and Pooh Bah of the Bursar's office, and is never caught out on a set of figures.

Well, then, what did this convenient and useful young man do when he was at last taken on the permanent staff? Pretty well everything, at first. In the Scullery, the Pantry, the Kitchen, the Pavilion. A lot of young men had gone into the services; those remaining had to turn their hand to all sorts of things. They had to 'bodge on as best they could'.

Jim soon gave evidence of competence in a variety of trades – decorating, naturally, but also plastering and carpentry. He drew the line at plumbing and electricals, but became a past-master at repairing windows. Indeed, he came to evolve his own measuring graph of a Headmaster's efficiency: a man with tight discipline gave Jim little to do in the way of repairs; a man with poor discipline was responsible for Jim running around so much with putty and glass and fatigue parties of miscreants that he began to wonder, as he said, 'who was having the punishment'.

However, he must have won the trust and respect of a succession of Heads, efficient and otherwise, because it became he who engaged the various firms of specialists for the respective jobs that needed doing. For the best part of forty years (the same length of service as his father before him) Jim was the Chief, mostly Only, Maintenance Man on the site.

He saw mains water come to the dormitories; he witnessed the transition from cesspit sanitation to that of septic tank; he presided over the changeover from solid fuel cooking to gas; he must have winced at the flak generated when the old food store was converted to the Staff Dining Room, and the grumbling kitchen staff had to trudge down the corridor to a new food store (where the present laundry is). 'There was a lot of running around' was his cryptic comment.

He took me on a conducted tour of the School, his memory batteries as full as if they had been charged the day before. Evocative names like the 'Paraffin Shed' and the 'Isolation Block' and the 'Engine House' tripped lightly off his tongue. The Fives Court and the Old Gym were pointed out. I was shown the remains of the 'Meat House', where pigs from the School's piggeries, after slaughtering – on site – were kept cool.

It was Commander Westall, I was told, who had put up the tennis courts at the front of the School, and Governors and their families used to come regularly to play and socialise in the warm summers of memory of the late 1930s, while the storm clouds of Appeasement and Nazi aggression billowed on a distant horizon.

I was introduced to the mystery of the Communal Bath – another of Westall's installations – where the old TV room was, beside the entrance to the Common Room. It is now an annexe to the Common Room, with a range of pigeon holes for Staff correspondence. 'The bath was never used,' said Jim. He doesn't know why. And he doesn't know what happened to it.

Did too many parents object to it? But then why would they, if they were prepared to accept communal showers and a communal swimming pool, where, I have been assured, swimming costumes were once deemed unnecessary? Then again, perhaps they might have argued that showers sluiced away the dirt at once, whereas a communal bath allowed a choice mixture of stale sweat and mud to form on its surface. Or was it simply a question of cost: the School's facilities could not meet the demands of such a huge vessel. Had Westall been overspending again?

From unfilled plugholes to overfilled pigeonholes – quite a transition.

Jim's memory was far from exhausted. I was regaled with sparkling nuggets of esoteric information. For instance, the generator that provided the School's electricity before the War had been made by 'Spence, of Honiton'. The septic tank was a 'Klargester'. (I bet you couldn't drop the name of a make of septic tank casually into the conversation. Well, now you can.) The School's crockery used to be delivered in barrels packed with straw to Filleigh Station. ('I used to have to sign for the stuff.') Apparently the previous china had been 'Grindley Hotel Ware', and was very heavy, with the School crest on it. (Was this Westall pushing the boat out once more? I have in the Archive a School cap from his time, with the name 'Harrods' inside the crown.)

Did you know that the School used to invite village children for Christmas parties? It was Mrs Harries actually. Hands up anyone who knew that the School once had its own petrol pump. Has it ever occurred to you that there might be a well underneath the floor of the present tuck shop? Well, there is. There is another one too, outside the Kitchen Manager's Office.

Which brings me rather neatly to the Kitchen Manager herself, Sylvia Ridd. Why? Because Jim remembers her starting work at the School, as a housemaid to the Headmaster, Mr Stephens, in 1961. Sylvia and Mr Stephens exchanged Christmas cards each year after he left, and continued to do so right up to the time Stephens died, only recently, aged ninety-two.

Jim's memory is so long that he goes back even before Gerald, who has worked at the School for over fifty years. Gerald must be so well known to so many old members of the School that there is almost a case for revamping the entire calendar of the School's history, to divide time into BG and AG – 'before Gerald' and 'after Gerald'. Jim remembers Gerald coming to the School as a lad of fifteen, in 1949.

Going back further still, he remembers, curiously, one of our two literary giants, Brian Aldiss. I had asked him if there were any boys he called particularly to mind, and he came out with this name. Naturally, I concluded that it was because of his literary talent, but Jim said no; he knew nothing of that at the time. It was simply that 'he sort of stuck out'. Which may be pleasing, if a little mystifying, to Mr Aldiss – unless both were privy to a deep secret that they still wish to maintain.

Jim was understandably proud of his record of carpentry. Under the guidance of a teacher, Mr Davey, he helped to make the huge dining tables that still grace the Dining Hall. Mr Davey was also responsible for many of the honours boards on the walls, no doubt with Jim's help too. A small plaque in the Hall records this achievement.

Mr Davey left in 1967. Maybe it is not entirely coincidence that Jim got a rise the following year. Quite by chance, while on another search errand, I came across a minute of a Governors' Meeting for that year, which recorded the agreement to grant a rise of £2 a week to 'Hobbs' (very feudal), to bring his salary up to the princely sum of £15 a week.

Anyone who lived through the winter of 1947 has their memories of it, and Jim is no exception. Think of the problems he must have had to face, as the sole maintenance man in a place like West Buckland, in the middle of nowhere, with its primitive plumbing, medieval services, and neolithic levels of comfort. They were snowed up for three weeks. Nearly every cast iron radiator broke. Water came through the ceilings in dining rooms and dormitories. Boys walked to Stag's Head for bread. And so on and so on.

One final anecdote is a neat illustration of the constant state of undeclared warfare that exists between guardians and inmates of a country boarding school. The Swimming Bath, said Jim, used to serve also as a miniature range. Remember the Bath was open to the skies in those days. In order to protect surfaces, galvanised iron sheets were put up all round the paper targets. However, boys being what they are, the cadets decided that it was much more fun to shoot, not at the targets, but at the iron sheets. They probably enjoyed the warlike 'pinging' and whining that their rounds made, and had fun counting the holes. It was hopeless to try and nail the culprits.

So Sam Howells, the Headmaster at the time, got Jim to paint tiny red circles round all the existing holes in the iron sheets. The next time fresh holes appeared, all Sam had to do was read off the names of the cadets of that day's firing, and he had got his man – or men. It would have been child's play to a man of Sam's experience, cynicism, and low cunning to single out the criminal. And, in the unlikely event of his failing, it would have occasioned him little unease to cane the lot of them '*pour encourager les autres*'.

Having spent two or three hours in Jim's company, I was not surprised when he told me that he had got on pretty well with most of the Heads with whom he worked. And since there have been in this piece one or two implied criticisms of Mr Westall, it seems fitting to close with a comment of Jim's about him to his credit. (He was not employed here during Westall's actual term of office, but his father was, and most of his family, and he lived only up the road, and he had probably come as a boy to Mrs Harries' Christmas parties, so the comment is, I am sure, valid.)

I had ventured the suggestion that, with the number of domestic staff that Westall had in his house, he must have lived in some style. 'Oh, he did,' agreed Jim very readily. 'But he looked a Headmaster,' he said. 'Even when he went on the prowl of an evening, in his carpet slippers, he looked a Headmaster.'

Natural authority. A rare gift. Not even Winston Churchill looked a particularly authoritative figure in his siren suit. And no man is a hero to his valet. So Westall had something.

So did Jim – a natural dignity, an entertaining command of old Devon idiom, and a phenomenal memory. He enjoyed a gossip, but he did not say anything malicious. He was a delight to talk to.

Jim Hobbs (1940-1980).

Mr Davey, the teacher who made all the magnificent dining tables in the Karslake, and also most of the honours boards. A plaque in the Karslake records this achievement.

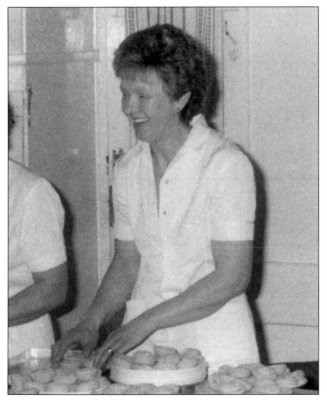

Sylvia Ridd, who came to work for Mr Stephens in 1961, and is still here.

Gerald (1949-) For over fifty years, the School has been his life. Like Jeeves, he needs no other name; he is universal and immortal.

Brian Aldiss, WB's second literary celebrity, with the dubious stories he had buried in a biscuit tin while at school in order to escape discovery – and retribution. They had lain undisturbed for over fifty years, till members of the sixth form dug them up.

FOUND IT: Schoolboys swarm round Brian Aldiss with the find, a fragment of which is shown on the right. Picture: JOHN CHAPPLE

MN 95

Author's buried stories are found

by JONATHAN SMITH

RAUNCHY cartoons and stories penned more than 50 years ago by best-selling author Brian Aldiss have been unearthed in the grounds of a West-country public school.

Entombed in a circular biscuit tin, the early works, read on pain of expulsion by 1940s teenagers, were dug up yesterday by sixth formers from West Buckland School, North Devon.

The hunt was sparked after West Buckland old boy David Hussell told the WMN about the ritual burial of the book during World War Two.

After more than four hours searching with metal detectors, the tin – untouched since the author left the school to join the Army in 1943 – was uncovered and the time capsule opened as Mr Aldiss looked on.

In the battered Lyons Gala Night Assortment tin were an exercise book, a Latin vocabulary book and a collection of saucy French cartoons.

"I feel quite weak at the knees," said Mr Aldiss, as he cradled the tin and flicked through the stories penned in his youth out of sight of matron and schoolmasters.

"By the look of the tin and the place where it was hidden, I obviously kicked it deep into the rabbit hole. I'm amazed it's turned up."

However, the promised tales of sex and crime did not materialise. "I did write a lot of raunchier stories, but I've come to the conclusion that I must have burnt them before I left," he said.

But Mr Aldiss, 69, is unlikely to publish the stories, which include the titles A Delinquent's Delusions, Lunatic at Large and his drawing of a mad artist.

"Half-a-century is a long time in literature. What is in the past should stay in the past," he added.

Nick Reed, 17, was among the group of A-level students who made the discovery after removing a hedge and digging at least a foot into the earth.

"We pulled back the hedge and dug around a bit and the earth suddenly fell away and there it was," he said.

The WMN tracked Mr Aldiss's former school friend Mr Hussell, also 69, to his Newton Ferrers home near Plymouth and told him of the discovery. "It's wonderful," said the retired builders' merchant.

The 'Meat House', where pigs were hung in the cool after they had been reared, and slaughtered, in the School piggeries.

The School in winter, when, admittedly, it does not snow every year. Far from it.

Another winter view taken as recently as January, 1999.

Taking Equality Too Far

On 14 July 1945, the School played a cricket match against Filleigh C.C. The match ended in a tie; both sides were all out for 63.

School		Filleigh C.C.	
Westacott, b Brooks	4	W. Facey, b Barnes	2
Barnes, b Facey	2	G. Brooks, run out	6
Jewell, c and b Woodhouse	14	Woodhouse, lbw Barnes	0
Norris, b Brooks	0	Collins, b Norris	8
P. Griffiths, b Brooks	6	Hardy, b Barnes	0
Follett, b Brooks	0	A. Brooks, b Griffiths	25
Bendle, lbw Bond	2	Bond, c Minns, b Norris	1
Minns, run out	4	Toze, c Hussell, b Norris	1
Pile, lbw Facey	4	S. Facey, b Griffiths	1
Hussell, b Bond	0	Bray, not out	7
Badcock, not out	0	Hile, c and b Norris	3
Extras	27	Extras	9
TOTAL	63	TOTAL	63

[And 'Extras' was top scorer – in the whole game.]

Nicknames

Boarding schools were fertile ground for nicknames, probably because the inmates were in more intimate and lengthier contact with each other week by week.

As boarding has declined over the years, so has the frequency of nicknames. But I think there is more to it than that. It would be tempting to mutter in one's whiskers and grumble that 'things aren't what they used to be', that there aren't the 'characters' around any more that there used to be, that pupils are simply not as good at thinking up nicknames as they used to be.

That may or may not be so. I would cite only one tendency that has obtruded itself on to my vision of things, and that is the number of nicknames which have come about by the simple adding of the letter 'y' on to the surname. Thus we have 'Clarky' or 'Wardy' or 'Hicky' or whatever – which shows great paucity of imagination in my view. Miles away from those great nicknames which at first sight seem to have no logical connection with their 'owner' at all, but which, when you think about it, encapsulate him perfectly. By what verbal alchemy are such names born? Deep waters, Watson, deep waters.

I offer here a collection, many of which come from R.F. Delderfield's own researches in his book *Tales Out of School*, which I think bear repetition. The rest have come from my own readings in School magazines, and from quizzing staff and Old Boys. I suspect the best ones come from way back.

Rosie	Whipper	Waso	Grannie	Joelegs	Trunker
Tightass	Luigo	Flanky	Yahoo	Elsie	Beeswax
Butterfly	Yan	Bo	Claude	Budey	Stallio
Ego	Mock	Guz	Lash	Hibou	Squeen
Gobber	Crabby	Vinegar	Brozer	Gonk	Clank
The Aph	Cap'n	Frank	Bouncer	Tuft	Mugsy
Piggy	Flea	Lurch	Eggy	Dido	Chimp
Aggy	Fry	Legweak	Inky	Jasper	Ernie
Judy	Tot	Horace	Harry	Jack	Pug
Bulldog	Yogi	Tuppence	Doc	Horsey	Doll's Eyes
Joppa	Titus	Matey	Bruiser	Chicken	Noller
Monkey	Crasher	Daly Boy	Beer	Phump	Fla Fa
Boggy	Manty	Reekie	Granny	Uncle Tom	Baby
Hobbo	Speigal	Snowball	Pop	Puck	

The *Register* No. 230 was the first edition of the School magazine to be printed after the outbreak of the Second World War. Its sole acknowledgement of this fact – in a publication of 27 pages – was the printing of a list of 'members of the School' who were 'serving in some branch of H.M. Forces'. It did not even claim that the list was complete or accurate.

There were seven and a half pages of lists of staff and pupils, one on births, marriages and deaths, two on the Phoenix Society, and twelve on cricket.

[I don't know what that shows you, but, whatever it is, it just shows you.]

BEING PROVED RIGHT

When you dig a mass of jumbled school archive material straight out of the loft, or the cupboard, or the bottom of the drawer, it is pretty obvious what you have to do with it in the first stages – after you have blown off the dust. Simple classifications like visual and documentary, sporting and academic, public and private records, and so on.

Then you split it up further – photos of cricket, rugby, football teams – all those hundreds of folded arms, tight jaws, steely eyes, and neatly-tied laces. Athletics teams with incredibly long and narrow legs. Cadet groups in straightjacket uniforms. Every young face so deadly serious.

The written material follows a similar pattern of arrangement – prospectuses, speech day programmes, play bills, inspection reports, confidential records on individuals, balance sheets – and correspondence. A lot of correspondence.

Among the greatest generators of letters were, predictably, headmasters. The subjects of their letters are equally predictable – testimonials for pupils hoping to go to university ('Benbow's assessment of his own abilities does not always coincide with that of his teachers'); breaking unwelcome news to parents ('it is with much regret that I must inform you that your son's continued attendance at this school has been rendered impossible by virtue of his incorrigible propensity for larceny'); thanking the visiting speaker at speech day ('the boys followed your enthralling speech with great interest; indeed it would be not too much to say that they hung upon your every word').

But every so often you come across something that defies classification. Among the correspondence of a headmaster of the post-war period (post-1945, that is) I found a letter from Messrs. Thomas De La Rue Company Limited – the 'Security Division', all about fountain pens. Yes, fountain pens. Well, one particular fountain pen, to be precise. It remains a mystery what connection a fountain pen has with the Security Division.

The letter was signed by the De La Rue Archivist – which naturally made it jump out of the page at me.

Mr Newman, the Archivist, was answering a query put by the Headmaster, though he does not say in his reply what the query was. What he does do is give information about what seems to be the very first fountain pen, which he says his firm advertised in the *Argosy* magazine of 1881. To wit, 'an Anti-Stylographic nibbed pen, patented by Hearson, a self-feeding reservoir penholder carrying a pen with ordinary nibs'. It preserved 'the usual characteristics of

the handwriting', it wrote 'like an ordinary pen', it contained enough ink 'to last several days', and it could be 'carried in the pocket without danger of leakage'. Such a treasure could be obtained for the modest sum of two shillings and sixpence (twelve and a half pence), or the 'desk size' for three shillings and sixpence (fifteen and a half pence).

Messrs. De Le Rue had purchased the original patent from Professor T.A. Hearson, and were marketing the pen as 'the first practical fountain pen'.

Mr Newman admitted that there had been, many years prior to 1881, a stylus type of fountain pen, patented by Joseph Bramah in 1809, and even quoted the patent number. But he points out that their pen was the first to use a device that permitted the use of a normal nib, and so was the first proper fountain pen. He calls up for support the big guns of the *Encylopaedia Britannica*.

He trusted that 'this information' would 'be of assistance' to the Headmaster. The Headmaster wrote back by return of post to thank Mr Newman, to say that he was 'pleased to know' that Mr Newman's information 'confirms our impression'.

All of which goes to show that you learn something new every day. Did you know that the first nib fountain pen came into production in 1881? Or that there had been a stylus type of fountain pen as early as 1809? I bet you didn't. Come to that, did you know the difference between a stylo pen and a nib pen? No, neither did I; I had to look it up. You can do the same; any decent dictionary will tell you.

But think. If Mr Newman was right, a minor revolution took place in the 1880s. From then on, no more continuous dipping and blotting – for those who could afford the new gadget – and at twelve and a half pence, it wouldn't break many domestic banks in the middle class at least. Think of all those diplomats who in future could sign the international treaties with their own pens, and they needed to rely on obsequious secretaries only to press the portentous half-moon blotters on their blue ink or violet ink or black ink – or whatever colour their whim had induced them to insert into their new devices.

Think of Toad, who could add yet another item to his pockets – to go with his 'pocket-book, money, keys, watch, matches, pencil case – all that makes life worth living, all that distinguishes the many-pocketed animal, the lord of creation, from the inferior one-pocketed or no-pocketed productions that hop or trip about permissively, unequipped for the real contest'.

Think of all those swank-pot schoolboys, who could conjure this latest invention out of doting parents, and impress their wondering classmates. (I remember cutting a similar dash just after the War, because a distant uncle who was in 'business' of some kind or other gave me one of the very first ball-point pens.) Had Billy Bunter flashed one about? Had a rich uncle sent him this unexpected prize in a parcel instead of the usual, and longed-for, postal order? He probably sold it to Coker of the Fifth in order to buy cream buns at the tuck shop.

Which brings me conveniently back to School, and so to the question which still needs to be answered. What on earth had the Headmaster said in his original letter? What had prompted his enquiry?

Had he inherited one from a grandparent? Had he come across one in a junk shop? No car boot sales in those days; no antiques road shows; no bring and buy – you went to junk shops.

Had the problem sprung from a controversial crossword clue in *The Times* – a controversy which had threatened to divide the entire common room from top to bottom?

'Eight letters – it's got to be "fountain".'

'Nonsense – it's "anti-stylo". It says "early", doesn't it?' (Science teacher – has a passion for observation and deduction.)

'My dear fellow, I know this man's method; he's been setting crosswords for thirty years. He wouldn't use such a word.' (Head of Classics – stickler for style.)

'You're all wrong. Who ever heard of fountain pens of any type going back that far? We still have to put up with ink wells even now. Still living in the eighteenth century, like the whole of education.' (Art teacher – modernist.)

Or again – was the Headmaster, having carelessly let slip an off-the-cuff piece of guesswork about the history of pens, involved in an exchange of remarks with a classroom swot? 'If you'll forgive me saying so, sir, the *Encyclopaedia Britannica* refers in the latest edition to . . .'

So there was only one way to settle this. He would write to the highest authority he could find.

And back had come the answer, vindicating him to the hilt. No wonder he was 'pleased to know'. That would put Four-Eyes Taplow in his place.

You can't win 'em all, but it is very nice when you win even one.

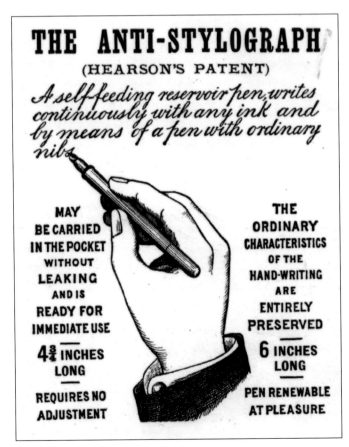

An advert for an early fountain pen.

On the back of this photo, in Headmaster Westall's (1934-39) tiny writing, are the words 'Drawing Office'.

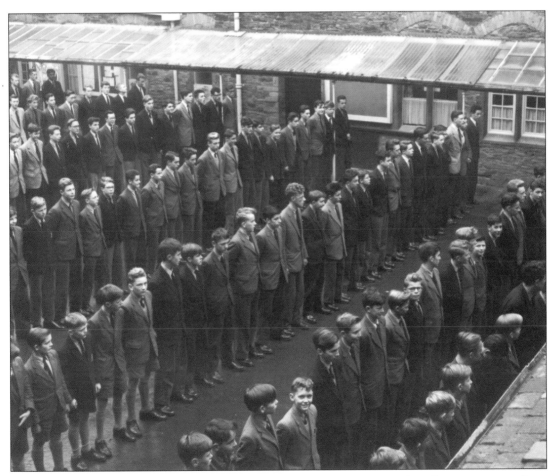

An assembly in the Quadrangle. Hair-do's are tidy, lines are straight, shoes are very clean indeed. They shine even at this distance.

A workshop. The pullovers, turn-ups, and sleek hair-do's would appear to place it in anywhere between the late thirties and mid-fifties.

A woodwork shop. The only person wearing an overall is the only one not doing any actual work – the teacher.

❀ WHAT DO GOVERNORS DO?

Ah, you may well ask. A lot of people have some idea of what governors are; but ask them what governors do, and you may find them up against it.

Part of the trouble stems from the fact that, unlike teachers, doctors, navvies, lawyers, shop assistants and till operators, you don't actually see them when they are governing. Their work has become a kind of rarefied mystery. You may easily see the result of their work, but you can rarely watch the work actually being 'worked', if you see what I mean. In this, governors share the same *modus operandi* with cardinals, political party chairmen, judges in chambers, secret agents, poets, philosophers and hired assassins.

Because of this mystery, you would expect governors to be shy, solitary creatures, like badgers, creeping along a misty hedgerow of an early morning or late evening. Or making rare appearances in the West Country like the Lesser Fantailed Moorland Mud Scrambler. You could almost imagine letters to The *Times* – 'caught sight of a governor this morning – in a playground – in early May. Is this a record?'

But no – they do manifest themselves from time to time – sightings have been noted at School fêtes, C.C.F. inspections, V.I.P. visits, and so on. They are usually to be seen in processions, at receptions and on platforms. So they are both public and gregarious. It is a curious fact that, if you saw a governor by himself (or herself – there are authenticated instances of the female of the species), you would probably have no idea who he or she was, unless he or she introduced himself – or herself. But *en bloc* they are instantly recognisable. They do not appear frequently, much less regularly, but it is not thought that they have any particular objection to so appearing. Perhaps it is because they do not get asked very often.

The most predictable occasion is of course Speech Day. You can recognise them at once because they are the slowest movers, they stay in line, they climb platform steps with great care, and they descend at the end as if the steps were an obstacle course. This is because of one of the great unwritten laws of Being a Governor: never, never be seen to collapse up a set of steps, or fall down one. It is not only because most of their actions are being watched by hundreds of curious or critical eyes; it is because nobody makes any excuse for governors. Teachers can trip over their gowns as they stride in, and that's a bit of a laugh, and we can pull old Jumbo's leg about it tomorrow; prizewinners from the Second Forms can stumble as they mount to the platform and be practically catapulted into the bosom of the Chief Guest, and the joke is at the expense of the Chief Guest, not the stumbler; but if a governor makes one tiny physical mistake, it's a hoot, and he's a pompous old buffer who should have been pensioned off years ago. (Oddly, it is a fact that governors, on the whole, do not seem to be very young.)

Most governors deal with this problem, understandably, by doing as little as possible, on the reasonable grounds that the less you do, the less you can get wrong. So, in between getting up on to the platform at the start, and coming down from it at the end, they do practically nothing. They have mastered the art of remaining absolutely still for hours at a time. Once the skirts and handbags and the trouser creases and cuffs have been given their final adjustment, they can, in an instant, congeal into parodies of Rodin. They have developed a built-in alarm clock which jolts them into consciousness at the end, after the School Captain has staggered through his short, well-memorised, impromptu Vote of Thanks to the Chief Guest. (One darkly suspects that there is a sub-committee of the Governing Body which takes new members aside and trains them in this esoteric art – a sort of Public Yoga.)

Perhaps one of the by-products of their being on public view is that they are usually pretty well dressed – have you noticed? Or it may be, of course, that it is only well-dressed people who are invited to become governors in the first place.

Which brings one to the business of qualifications. What do you need to be, or to have done? Ah – once again – you may well ask.

I persuaded a couple of colleagues to try this out on their junior classes, and their answers displayed the mixture of nonsense, wild inaccuracy, random shrewdness, and lunatic aptness which is often associated with children's views of the world. In answer to the question 'What qualifications do governors need?' there were the predictable suggestions that they needed to be an ex-pupil or an ex-teacher. Which is reasonable, and maybe not far wrong. This is the sort of place you need to be inured to; you might find it hard to come 'cold', as it were, from somewhere else. The Hapsburg Emperor once said to someone who aspired to royalty, 'Nobody, if he knew what it entailed, would really want to be an emperor; you have to be born to it.'

Another first-form philosopher suggested that it would be a fine thing if a potential governor had a 'good school record'. One is tempted to wonder how many governors can place their hand over their heart and claim that. One pupil democrat thought they were elected by parents – which has a fair bit of mileage in it. (Rather like the answer Gandhi gave to the question 'What do you think of Western Civilisation?' – 'I think it would be quite a good idea.')

It says a good deal for the common sense of these eleven-year-olds that a lot of them felt that a degree would be a useful aid. And several suggested that it should be associated with business, finance, law, and so on. Governors may find that analysis flattering, I don't know. But I don't think they would find flattering the alternative opinion that they should 'have office and filing qualifications' – though the child in question went on to say that they should also be 'liked'.

It says a good deal also for the perception of the awesome authority of the Headmaster that one theory advocated that candidates should 'go through a course and see what the Headmaster thinks of you'. At which many a harassed headmaster may secretly whisper to himself, 'If only, if only…' Others, not so awestruck by the man in the hot seat, said that governors were 'promoted from headmaster or headmistress'. (Like being kicked upstairs?) So being a headmaster was not all that wonderful.

There was one cynic. In answer to the question – which I repeat in case you have forgotten it by this time – 'What qualifications do governors need?' – he said, 'None.'

How many governors would be prepared to go into the debating arena against him?

The highest demands made came from the child who said, 'They need to be a lord and have a degree in English.' Bearing in mind the number of independent schools in the country, and the average I.Q. of the House of Peers, one might be forgiven for wondering how there can be enough to go around.

But, as with most surveys of juvenile opinion, there is often one still small voice almost drowned by the more strident certainties. Someone tentatively proposed that one became a governor by 'being a good person for the school'. That, I think, takes a bit of beating.

Interesting, though, how governors themselves seem to be quite taken with this business of qualifications. Titles and styles of address too. No school governing body worth its salt is without its 'Sirs' and its 'Very Revds' and its 'Major-Gens'. Another useful ingredient is a couple of double-barrels. And, when it comes to the initials after the name, that's when they go to town. In the years following the War, D.S.Os and M.Cs abounded. Bit more difficult these days, unless the governor has survived, and distinguished himself in, one of the many obscure little wars in places like Malaysia or Kenya or Cyprus – and even those were over forty years ago. (No wonder they have to watch it going up the steps.) We have to look

to places like Ulster or the Falklands now for bemedalled veterans with any lingering traces of Douglas Fairbanks left in them.

An M.P. or a J.P. was, and is, always a worthwhile embellishment to any governing body. But the best thing to do is to print, after your name, some unbelievably long acronym that only some other holder of it would understand. Hence, we finish with something like 'Sir Jonathan Willoughby-Smythe, M.B.E., Tech. D.(U.S.A.), Inst. Tog. St. Ump, Res. (Hons.) sst.com.uk.'

All this may stem, not from pomposity, but from a passion for formality – which is where we came in with the matter of dress. Is it that people tend to become formal because they have been chosen as governors, or do they become governors because they have exhibited the required level of respect for formality?

It is not only in dress too that one sees it. Look at their proceedings. They are never 'pleased to hear about' something; they 'welcome' it. They are not hopping mad about a deficit from the tuck shop fund; they 'deplore' it. They do not think the Bursar's resignation is a damned shame; they 'receive it with regret'. They do not think that spending the credit balance of the building fund on new cricket nets is a smashing idea; they 'heartily endorse it'.

It is not exactly circuitous English, but it is a sort of unreal English. They do this in aeroplanes and railway trains, too. You are not 'told' anything; you are 'informed'. You do not 'buy' things; you 'purchase' them. In fact you don't even purchase 'things'; you purchase 'items' or 'commodities'.

It becomes difficult to maintain this stiffness of language when it comes to actual discussion of concrete problems – often literally concrete problems like crumbling stonework or drain linings. Glance through any twenty or thirty pages of Governors' Minutes, and you will be struck by how much time is taken up with these mundane matters which admit of no circumlocution at all. No matter how you look at it, a kitchen stove is a kitchen stove; a cesspit is a cesspit. Thank God that governors have not descended to the tortuous level of jargon like that of, say, the Pentagon, where 'impaired combat personnel' has to serve for 'wounded soldiers'.

The winter of 1947 wreaked havoc with this formalism, as it wreaked havoc with so many things. The Minutes recorded that the blockage of snow was so bad that 'gangs' of boys had had to walk to Stag's Head in order to get bread, meat and the post. Note – not 'groups' of boys, nor even 'detachments' or 'details', but 'gangs'. But it took the worst winter of the century to cause the mask to slip.

A man once went to spend some time in a monastery – on retreat in fact. He was concerned about the conversation he would have to share at the refectory table in the evening; he was not a particularly religious or knowledgeable chap and he did not know how he would keep up with arcane observations on the Trinity or discussion of the latest pastoral pronouncement from His Holiness. He need not have worried; the brothers spent the entire meal discussing football.

So the Minutes of Governors' meetings are chock full, not of educational philosophy or the virtues of language laboratories, but of dining-room chairs, drains, coal deliveries, maintenance men's wages, dry rot in the Headmaster's house, water in the dormitories, corrosion in the pipes, chlorination plants and septic tanks.

Now and again they bring up bank balances and government legislation and staff salaries. And once in a while they actually discuss pupil numbers and exam results. Perhaps those junior analysts who said that governors needed degrees in business and law and finance were not far wrong after all. Though they might have added civil engineering and surveying.

So where do they fit into the overall scheme of things? Do they run the place? If they don't, who does? Is it the Headmaster? Who can dismiss whom? Heads have been asked for their resignation before now. But it is hard, I should think, for a head to ask for a governor's resignation. Things don't work like that. After all, the Queen has the legal authority to dismiss the Prime Minister, and the Prime Minister cannot dismiss the Queen; but there is little doubt as to who is running the country.

Then again, a prime minister might be able to stay in office even though the monarch disapproves of nearly everything he does, but I wonder how long a head would remain if the board of governors disapproved of what he did.

And what about the man who controls the finances – the Bursar? Parliament's powers grew as they gradually gained control over the purse-strings. Does that put the Bursar beyond correction?

Analysis of true power is a fascinating topic. Wherein lies the ultimate authority? Who has the power to influence more lives that anyone else on a school campus? The Headmaster? The Governors? The Bursar? They are the obvious candidates. But true power is an elusive thing to track down. Is it the School Secretary? Is it the Headmaster's wife? Is it the Chief Caretaker, who, at the flick of a switch in the central heating system, has the power (in every sense) to make everybody's life a misery? Is it the Catering Manager, who, if she has an off day, can lay us all low with food poisoning? Is it the lazy pupil, who, by calculated inertia (at which he is a past master), can ruin the exam. result prognostications, and force the School prospectus to be rewritten? To say nothing of ruining Speech Day.

One can speculate endlessly, and get nowhere. One ends by being forced to admit lamely that governors fit in somewhere, and are necessary, but one is not quite sure where or how.

After having thought about it for some time, I offer the analogy of parents. Are governors like parents? Think for a moment. There is no universally recognised training system or qualification for either of them. Despite what those children I quoted put on their answer papers, there is in fact no means by which a governor can say, 'Make way; I am a trained governor.' Neither can a parent. Both parents and governors are unpaid, unsung, and unpublicised – unless they make mistakes or commit offences. There are competitions for 'Sportsman of the Year' and 'Best Actor of the Year', but none for 'Parent of the Year' or 'Governor of the Year'. But let one parent or one governor make a bloomer or do something wrong, and the tabloid press will shriek 'Bully of the Year' or 'Buffer of the Year' or whatever.

Both get accused, at various times, of being quaint, infuriating, stuffy, unfair, short-sighted, inefficient, negligent, pompous, old-fashioned spoilsports. Yet both would get noticed most easily if they were not there. Neither set out to be what they became; it just sort of happened. And both no doubt must have wondered at times what they had let themselves in for.

But nobody forced them to do it. Which brings us full circle – what do they do? It is altogether too fanciful to suggest this? Parents are not teachers, doctors, dentists, therapists or games coaches; they just do everything else. By the same token, governors do not run the accounts, the classes, the exams., the playing fields, the dormitories, the kitchens or the drains; they just do everything else. And they do it presumably, because, like parents, they want to.

And they do it because, as that perceptive young analyst observed, they are each 'a good person for the School'.

A typical clutch of Governors – in this case from the 1940s. *Left to right:* Col. C. Wheeler, D.S.O., Capt. F.G. Glossop, R.N., Messrs. H.G. Pearce, F.H. Shelley, F.J. Loosemore, the Revd E.C. Harries, Mr E.J. Taylor, Mr W.T. Buckingham, J.P., Preb. I.L. Gregory, Mr S. E. Howells (Headmaster), and Col. G.B. Oerton, T.D., D.L.

A glorious view of the moorland surroundings of the School. There cannot be many schools with a setting like this. Even many who started like this became squeezed by later building. Small wonder the Governors stressed it in their prospectuses.

A register exists recording the attendance (or not) of Governors at various meetings and committees between 1952 and 1966. Just like the pupils. [But I bet they didn't get detention for truanting.]

We Are Not Amused

On 20 November 1956, the land agent for Lord Fortescue, Mr J.M.B. Mackie (M.A., F.R.I.C.S., F.L.A.S.), wrote a letter to the Headmaster, Mr L.W. Stephens, about what might be described as some burning issues:

'Lord Fortescue has instructed me to write to you about the fire which occurred at Lower Pitt Farm, East Buckland and burnt down a hay shed there.

I understand that it has now been established that this fire was caused by two boys from your school.

A very serious view is taken of this and I must ask you to make it quite clear to the school that all buildings on the Fortescue Estates are strictly out of bounds.

I understand from a number of tenants on the Estate that they have had to warn boys off their farms because of the nuisance which they cause by leaving gates open, etc.

While I am writing I would also mention the following matters but would stress there is no proof that the damage was caused by any of your boys:

A new asbestos roof at Blakewell was smashed within a few weeks of it being completed.

All the windows in the cottages at Embercombe were broken within a short time of them being put in order.

The old oak tree in front of Westacott farm was set on fire.

I understand that a minor fire occurred at East Buckland Mill last summer.

I have not raised these matters with you before but would like to bring them to your notice now.

I am quite sure that Lord Fortescue has no objection to the boys walking over the estate so long as they behave themselves in a proper manner but there seems little doubt, from what I have said above, the privilege seems to be somewhat abused.'

[Somewhat!]

A Somewhat Anonymous Pupil

'X.X. ZZZZZZZ has been a boarder here since +++++, ++++. He has never played a prominent part in the life of the school, academic or otherwise...He is not a hard worker, though he deludes himself that he is... He is in many ways a "dark horse" and a "lone wolf", if it is possible for this biological freak to be perpetrated: there is little to be said either in his favour or his disfavour socially in the school: he is no games player...he holds no post of responsibility, and does not appear likely to be made a prefect. His main hobbies are mechanical and electrical...and he enjoys taking things to pieces and (sometimes) putting them together again...'

(Extracts from a confidential report.)

It would be possible to read several things into this passage. Firstly, one could be shocked that even a selective extract from a confidential report should find its way into a miscellany like this. But, since every factor that could lead to any possible identification has been deleted, it would seem a pity to leave the remark about 'dark horse' and 'lone wolf' unrecorded.

Which leads on to the observation that could be made about the propensity of the teaching profession for making ironic remarks. That could lead in turn to an orgy of reminiscence among readers about cutting observations made upon their work or their play by sardonic schoolmasters – many of which are eminently quotable not only for their sharpness and their humour but for their accuracy.

Thirdly, it shows that teachers do not always see their geese as swans. When writing a report for a university admissions tutor, a certain amount of honesty must be evident, if the teacher is going to maintain any level of credibility with that admissions tutor in the future.

Or again, and this is not so evident from the passage above because several parts have been left out, a teacher will do his best to be fair and to give as rounded a picture as he can. The writer of this report was at pains more than once to say that the pupil was never in trouble, and that he played games, if not to a distinguished level, and so on. He did do his best.

It would be nice to be able to record that the subject of this report went on to become a captain of industry or a politician or the Archbishop of Canterbury, but, sadly, we don't know. Pity.

Cordy Wheeler

A Rare Man

It is given to very few people to save their School from extinction. To even fewer to do it twice.

When Cordy Wheeler died in 1972, his fellow-Governor, Michael Roberts, paid a touching and heartfelt tribute to him. He began by listing his many distinctions.

Then he went on, 'On two occasions he was instrumental in preventing the School closing down.' When J.B. Challen left in 1900, he took with him two-thirds of the boys to set up another school in Barnstaple, leaving only a rump of thirty-odd boys behind. The Directors (the School then was a private company) decided that there was no alternative to closure. Cordy Wheeler, Head Prefect, but only a pupil nevertheless, 'went to Lord Fortescue to plead with him to get them to change their minds' – apparently with success.

Barely seven years later, the School was in a bad way again, with mounting debts. The Directors again thought that closure seemed the only solution. 'Cordy disagreed, and succeeded, with the financial help of two Old Boys, Michael Snell and R.P. Chope, in getting them to change their minds and appoint Ernest Harries Headmaster.' (Cordy had worked with Harries at Blundell's, and thought he was the man to lead the School out of trouble.) Again, his courage was vindicated, and, as the School prospered under Harries' leadership, his judgment was vindicated as well.

Michael Roberts went on to describe Wheeler's tireless work as Chairman of Governors, in tackling the appalling backlog of vital repairs which had accumulated during the years of the War and of post-War austerity.

He paid tribute to his energy, his courage, his kindness (for instance in visiting retired old servants of the School), his leadership, his wisdom, his capacity for friendship, and his towering integrity. 'Seldom, if ever, has any school owed more to one man.'

[It is a pleasure to give a compliment; it is a pleasure to receive one. But there are times when it is an equal, and moving, pleasure to witness such a handsome, open-hearted compliment being paid by one person to another.]

Les Mots Justes

After having made contact with an Old Boy called R.N. Armstrong (1958-65) in connection with a book he had written (see 'A Lorry Load'), I received a letter from him about the author R.F. Delderfield. R.F.D., it seems was 'a frequent visitor' to the Phoenix Society.

'He spoke to us at a Phoenix Society Dinner one night and told us about a book he had just finished writing – a country saga. The American publisher had told him that his original title, *Portrait of a Patriot,* was unsuitable for them because "Patriots" in the U.S. are anti-British. Ronnie then asked us if we had any ideas for another title – long silence – until Armstrong stands up. I had been studying W.B. Yeats and the epitaph that he had written for himself seemed quite apt. "Cast a cold eye, on Life, on Death, Horseman Ride By!"

'Ronnie scribbled this on a packet of Woodbines and nobody thought any more of it for a month or two. Then I heard that he had used an adapted version (the original had already been used).

'I was invited to the presentation of the book at a hotel in Exeter and was given a signed copy – the first one off the press – which of course I still have. *A Horseman Riding By* – April, 1966 .. "remembering the occasion at West Buckland when you suggested the title". '

THE NEW LINEN ROOM ASSISTANT

Barbara Hollingsworth has kept the reply which she received from the Headmaster, in answer to her application, for twenty-five years. It makes interesting reading. It was handwritten by the Headmaster himself, George Ridding, and was dated 23 December 1974. Perhaps the School Secretary had packed up for the Christmas holidays. Or the School had hit a bad patch.

Certainly the best offer Mr Ridding could make barely exceeded fifty pence an hour by way of wages. For her projected thirty-two and a half hours a week ('to fit in with buses from South Molton'), Barbara was to receive £17.38. Though Mr Ridding did hold out the incentive that by the following September the rate would have gone up to £25.02. (I like the '.02'. I hope she didn't spend it all at once.)

Barbara Haywood (as she was then) was in no mind to bargain, or to complain. She had recently moved down to Devon with her parents when they came to retire, and was looking for a convenient job to tide her over while she looked for the kind of work she had been used to before the move. She had been in a busy office, with computers and so on, and 'down here there weren't computers much in 1975' – which seems to be the sort of gentle criticism which is typical of her. She saw the advert. in the *North Devon Journal Herald*, and applied. Mr Ridding offered her the job; she accepted.

And very soon she was beginning to regret it.

Laundering hundreds of boys' pants was 'quite a shock to the system'. She decided, 'I sha'n't stick this; two weeks and I shall be off.' She had only meant it to be a 'fill-in between office jobs' anyway.

That was twenty-five years ago. So something must have happened which surprised her. 'I felt at home here. I'd worked in my previous job for seventeen years, but I did a job and went home. Here it was different; I felt part and parcel of the place. I felt I belonged.'

The job certainly wasn't easy. There were four dormitories to run. Their inmates had to be kept clean, healthy and hygienic. Two clean shirts a week, and at least two clean pairs of socks and pants. A book was kept to check up on their regularity of clothing change. Every item of clothing had to be physically checked on coming in, on going out to the laundry (in Bideford), on coming back, and on re-distribution to the owners. And, including juniors and Prep., there were about 180 boarders on the books.

Comforts were few and far between, even as recently as twenty-five years ago. No sixth-former had a study, though 'I think there was a room for the Head Boy'. Dormitories had no carpets or heating. In cold weather some of the windows wouldn't shut properly, so Barbara stuffed the gaps with blankets. (The boys were at least allowed as many blankets as they wanted.) There were no curtains either.

Ice formed in the wash-basins. I queried this; wasn't this just one of the legends put about by loquacious Old Boys who wanted to show everyone how tough it had been? And how could the basins have ice in them first thing in the morning; surely that showed that there been water standing in them all night, and that was hardly hygienic, was it? A shrewd, incisive thrust of interrogation, I thought. Barbara dealt with it with disdainful ease.

No, she said. A lot of the taps dripped. The water from them steadily froze and went on to spread over the basin. Unwilling to give in so easily, I tried a rear-guard action: What about the maintenance staff? Shouldn't they have been doing something? Barbara shook her head.

'There was only one man to cover the whole School.'

I retreated in total disarray.

The Bursar's words came back to me. When I had asked him to say what would first come into his mind if he had to describe Barbara, he said, 'Gentle but firm.' I had been dealt with gently but firmly.

And that was how she treated the boys. A colleague told me, 'She's got a real gift with children.' A gift with colleagues too, apparently. The same lady readily admitted, 'Everything I've learnt here I've learnt from her.'

The boys needed somebody they could turn to and trust and rely on. 'You've got to remember,' said the same colleague, 'that, apart from Matron, we were almost the only women the boys saw regularly from beginning to end of term. We steered a lot of them through difficult times, right from their first day.' Barbara, she said, was always 'gentle and peace-making'.

She took further duties in her stride as they came along.

The advent of girls – was that difficult? No – they boarded them – only a few at first – at North Lodge, just past Filleigh old railway station, and fetched them to School in a minibus.

What about co-education as a whole – what was her opinion? 'That's a hard one. No thoughts too much on that.' Several times Barbara answered like this, not because she had no views, but because she had not thought them out sufficiently to feel able to express them as fairly as she would wish. She refused to demean our meeting, or herself, with glib, instant, snappy judgments.

Bearing in mind the colleague's comment about her kindness, and the spartan conditions of a quarter of a century ago, I asked her if she had ever felt sorry for the boarders.

After the briefest of pauses, she said, 'No. Because they always came across as quite a happy bunch.' Far from missing home, she reckoned, they usually seemed pleased to get back to the School after the holidays.

Curiously, the boys didn't jump for joy when heating was installed in the dormitories. 'They weren't all that bothered. It's the parents more than the children you have to do it for.' Nowadays, she admitted, they do complain if the heating goes off, or even down. But 'what you never have you never miss'; there were no grumbles in the bad old days.

When the headmaster of the time decided that the boys were getting a bit scruffy, Barbara was invited to become Clothing Matron, which must have given her further opportunity to spread her unobtrusive but invaluable influence. She saw at once that the important time for the boys' smartness was first thing in the morning, so she arranged to come into work at 8.30 instead of 9.00 – 'just to see them off'.

This is one the hallmarks, isn't it, of the good colleague; they always have time. Or, if they do not, they make it. Somebody else I asked to make a comment about her said, at once, 'Oh, kind. Gently kind, efficient.' Then he thought for a moment, and added, 'If you ask her to do you a favour, she never says anything else but "Certainly".'

This calm efficiency masked a variety of talents. In fact, as the first colleague remarked, 'She was over-qualified. Brilliant at figures.'

So the responsibilities multiplied, until she was officially recognised as Assistant Bursar – 'my right hand', said the Bursar. By the time she reached retirement, Barbara was responsible for the organisation of the cleaning of the entire campus, inside and outside; she supervised the provision of facilities for public functions; she exercised an overview of health and safety arrangements within her department; she ran the School laundry (still); she arranged the re-struc-

turing of accommodation for holiday guests and conferences and summer schools; she oversaw the running of a School outfitter's shop for clothing and sports gear. Not bad going for an ex-Linen Room Assistant. Good at figures all right.

Did any episodes stand out in her memory? In a place like West Buckland, it is hardly surprising that bad weather came to mind first. After a heavy snow-storm, Barbara had to come in on a Saturday morning, with some other willing souls, and clamber up into the loft over the present chapel, and, with buckets and shovels, move all the snow that had blown in above the ceiling. She remembers the Headmaster being around too. There was little demarcation in those days: 'You never asked if you should do this.' You just got on and did it.

She remembered turning the chapel and the careers room into temporary extra wards during an epidemic of 'flu'. She remembered two boys who stole musical instruments and who were caught trying to sell them to a second-hand shop in Barnstaple. She remembered a lot of 'nice foreign boys', who were happy to come in to talk. She remembered one obstinate little boy who persistently failed to make his bed. Even Barbara's usual remedy – stripping the bedding and making a nice pile of the sheets and blankets at the foot of the bed – had failed. Instead of coming to heel, this obstreperous little goblin had responded by tearing every button off his shirt. She remembered a particularly resourceful (and obviously hardened) young miscreant who, whenever he was due for the cane, came up into the dormitory and put on every pair of underpants he possessed.

Only twice did she venture a spontaneous verdict. Once, out of the blue, she observed, when talking about changes, 'It's a shame they don't say Grace now.' And, *à propos* of nothing in particular, she said, 'One underlying thing – it's always been a happy school.'

Barbara had obviously got a lot of happiness out of it, but it is equally clear that she had put a lot of happiness in, by her own dedication, professional pride, kindness, imagination and dignity.

'It's not like a job. It's a joy to come to work. After twenty-five years, I still feel the same.'

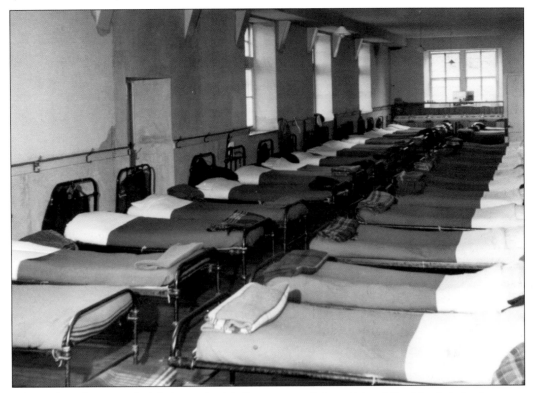

A later dormitory, probably from the 'sixties, or even later. At least the blankets had grown some colours by this time.

Compare the plumbing, soap dispensers, mirrors, and general brightness (and absence of ladders) with the awful Colditz barn in earlier photographs.

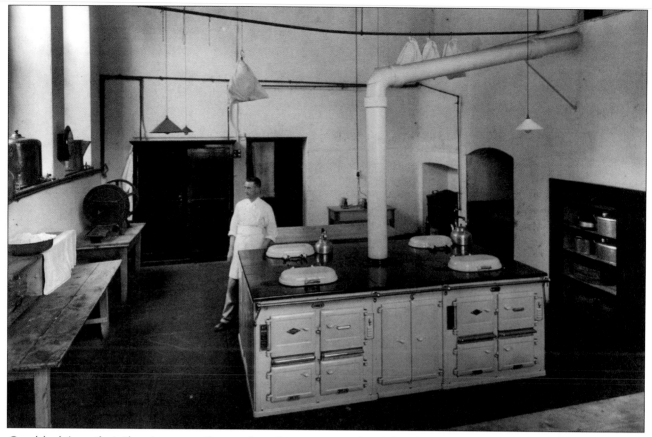

Gerald claims that the Aga was there when he came to the School in 1949. Gerald's record of service, incidentally, beats that of Mr Watson by nine years.

John Parker, the Chief Maintenance Engineer in the School, is master of so many trades that he can build an entire house from foundations to rooftops.

The Honest Schoolmaster

A teacher of Economics was so well aware that his lectures on warm afternoons after a heavy lunch could be soporific that he once went to sleep himself – during his own lecture.

Berwick Coates, the School Archivist, although he has taught History for a very long time, actually began his academic career teaching Swahili.

A Consummation Devoutly to be Wished

A young geography teacher made the mistake of attempting to combine the shepherding of a school party on a trip to India with his honeymoon. He spent most of the time suffering from a severe stomach upset and lost over two stone.

BRUISED FEELINGS

Those who write history have to decide, sooner or later, what their view of history is. For example, does history present a record of relentless progress or inexorable decline? Put another way, are things getting better all the time, or is it that things not only are not what they used to be; they never were. Is there a pattern discernible in it, as the Marxists, for instance, would have us believe? Or is it, as a distinguished Oxford historian, A.J.P. Taylor, put it, just one damn thing after another?

In the nineteenth century, the century which gave birth to the School, it was fashionable to see the history of England as one long march to the high plateau of achievement which Victorian times seemed to demonstrate. A chequered march, maybe, but a triumphant one nevertheless. The Industrial Revolution, the British Empire, the British Navy, the British form of constitutional government – these were the ultimate, the end, the last word – unique feats deserving the highest praise. No other nation or country, in their efforts to better themselves, could do better than aspire to emulate Britain.

It is a case of fondness and pride standing still, unchallenged, and curdling to become complaceny and arrogance.

Similarly, in the history of any other institution, while pride in achievement has its place, and rightly so, one must guard against complacency. West Buckland in the year 2000, for all its praiseworthy successes, does not necessarily represent the very last word in education; and the history of its past should not imply an endless, unbroken chronicle of progress, happiness, high endeavour and good relations. As Oliver Cromwell insisted, there are warts on the face too.

Three examples will serve to illustrate this.

In the spring of this year, a lady left the domestic staff in a state of considerable unhappiness. It would be an intrusion to list the details, and however many people I spoke to in order to get a rounded picture of the matter, I should never get right to the 'truth', if such a 'truth' exists. The unfortunate situation has arisen through a combination of circumstances both in the School and outside it, both through her own feelings and through the decisions of others (decisions taken no doubt with the best interests of the School at heart, as those deciders see it). And it would be safe to guess too that there has been the usual dose of misunderstanding stirred in.

Whatever the causes, the lady left, and left with many regrets and hurt feelings.

Then again, just over thirty years ago, there was a change of headmaster. Within months, there was trouble. Never mind 'who started it'; trying to apportion 'blame' – if indeed 'blame' is the right word anyway – would be like trying to find out who began a primary school playground punch-up, and just as unedifying. Suffice it to say that, before the crisis was over – and it was some crisis – there had been a mass resignation of a clutch of governors; the Headmaster himself had resigned, and been reinstated; and, as I discovered from a stray letter I came across in a mixed box of papers, one long-term supporter and benefactor of the School had, allegedly, stated that he 'did not intend to set foot in the place again'.

However justified the feelings of these participants may have been, it must, from the School's point of view, be regarded as a very regrettable episode.

Finally, an example from a hundred years ago. The Headmaster, Mr J.B. Challen, who had come in 1895 with a glowing record, resigned and left, at the end of 1899. Nothing in the surviving documents gives any advance warning of this sudden rift. On the contrary, the School's historian, Jon Edmunds, points out that for the four previous years, fulsome compliments had been paid on prize days to Mr Challen's stewardship. He was a brilliant sportsman too. It was during his Headship that the School produced the boy who became arguably the School's greatest all-round scholar-sportsman, William Stradling. Certainly the greatest in its first fifty or sixty years. (By a curious, if macabre, coincidence, both Challen and Stradling died within twelve months of each other, 1936-37.)

The only hint comes in the Governors' Minutes, which referred to complaints by boys and parents about meals and other matters connected with the general running of the School. Later on, the Minutes recorded the Governors' verdict that, after examing these complaints, they did not think there was a great deal of substance in them. Then, inexplicably, they decided, unanimously, that, under the circumstances, they had no option but to ask for Mr Challen's resignation. They would not even tell Challen, when he asked, the grounds on which they had based this draconian decision. Challen duly resigned. Not only did he leave; he took two-thirds of the boys with him to start another school in Barnstaple.

The whole episode bristles with oddities. Why did the complaints take so long to materialise? Why did they arise at all, after the previous glowing testimonials to Mr and Mrs Challen? Why did the Governors decide to ask for Challen's resignation after they had formed the opinion that there was little substance to the complaints? And why – if so many boys and parents were fed up with the food and the conditions – did so many boys go with Challen to Barnstaple? Why were so many parents content to let them go?

We shall never know. But clearly there must have been a lot of upset people in and around West Buckland at the end of 1899.

If one were to dig around, one could no doubt find plenty more examples of controversy. But digging around usually produces a great deal of dirt. And dirt is not its own justification.

Why then produce these three?

Because they serve to show that West Buckland, if one may personify it for a moment, is human. It does not pursue a smooth course along an unbroken yellow brick road of charm and nostalgia and jolly old school tie. Like any person of mature years, it has episodes and events in its career which are a source of sorrow, pain and regret. They are there, in the record, and there is nothing one can do about it.

That is not to say that one should dwell on them. Nor should one attempt to pretend they didn't happen. Like any mature person, the School has to live with these things. Live with them, and learn from them. And, in its effort to promote the happiness of all those within its walls, try to make sure that they don't happen again.

Coming Out of the Woodwork

When the old dormitories were converted into the new English, Drama, and Music Departments, the rooms were completely gutted. This involved, among other things, ripping out all the old wainscots. And what should the builders find but hundreds of cigarette ends, pinched out and stuffed down through gaps in the plaster over the years by satisfied, smug, and very resourceful pupils after they had finished their last furtive puffs of the day.

Interesting now for the student of ancient brands. There they were – Player's 'Weights', Wills' 'Woodbines', 'de Reszke'. Interestingly, mostly filter-tipped too. Were those distant late-night puffers prey to the once-fashionable belief that if you smoked filter cigarettes the risk of lung disease was that much less?

And what luck they all enjoyed. Think of the risk! In all those years, not one cigarette end smouldered long enough to set off the others and so send up the entire wainscot in flames.

Did anybody ever contemplate the danger? I doubt it. Criminals only engage in their crimes if they think there will be no retribution. Secondly, any act of defiance has a trick of eroding common sense. And thirdly, whatever the outcome, the pleasure and satisfaction to be derived convinced them that it was all 'worth de Reszke'.

Alan Rogers, the Systems Manager in the IT Department, goes on holiday with his wife to the United States. Nothing unusual in that. But there is something unusual in how they spend their holidays: they chase tornadoes across Texas and Oklahoma and other states nearby.

❀ A Cut Above the Average ❀

A school blazer is – well, a school blazer, wouldn't you say? Think of the times you have cast a casual glance into school outfitters' windows; school blazers all look pretty much the same, don't they? Apart from the obvious differences in colour and pocket badge. It may be that some of you have bought these garments for your offspring, but I would bet that the only thing that stays in your memory from the experience is the shock to the system on discovering the price.

Well, I have to inform you that school blazers are not all the same – not by a long chalk. (Sorry about the pun. Pun? School blazer – chalk – classrooms?… Oh, never mind.) How do I know this? Because archivists get all sorts of old things handed in to them. And recently I was given some school clothing belonging to a boy who had attended the School in the 1920s.

First the cap. (Yes, yes, I know, I started by talking about blazers; they are coming in a minute.) Only a couple of moth-holes betrayed its age. Turn it inside out and you find a lining of silk – silk! The supplier's label was still clear – Harrod's, no less. Perhaps there were not that many school outfitters available in those days. Somebody ought to do a monograph on them – you know, lavishly illustrated with colour fold-outs of gym slips and rugger shorts, and supplements on makers' labels and types of gold thread for badges, all cross-referenced to events and personalities of the period in question – the very latest thing for the coffee tables of with-it parents. A splendid talking-point for those little Riesling get-togethers of 75 of their best friends before they fly off to the Seychelles or Samoa for the February half-term.

Then the blazer badge – light years away from the mass-produced machine embroidery of today. It has all been done by hand, in fine gold- and silver-coloured wire, probably copper-based. The owner of this blazer also had two images of crossed rifles hand-embroidered on his cuff. Workmanship of this standard would have taken a skilled person a whole day to complete.

It took a long time to produce a blazer too. Although it was not lined, it had 'run and fell' seaming, which meant that there were no raw edges exposed, and each seam was sewn three times altogether. This made a garment which was so stable that the cloth would disintegrate before the seams split. And remember we are talking about an item of clothing which is over seventy years old. A boy could wear it today. (Not that he would, but he could.)

A great give-away in modern blazers is the pockets. It is there that they fray first. In our old blazer there were hand-sewn circles of wool felt reinforcing the pockets on the inside where the stitching starts and finishes. It is a detail almost of an *haute couture* garment today.

Care and imagination had been shown too in the cut of the pockets' shape. None of your modern uniform rectangular block. Corners were well rounded, and had a narrower top opening, so that the pocket resembled a sort of half-filled sack. Better for security, I should think.

A garment like this was made to last. Evidence inside the shell of the blazer showed that it had generous seam allowances, to cater for the future growth of the wearer in height and girth. Other evidence showed that such alterations had in fact been made, and more than once.

Now, you may well ask at this stage, how come one of your common or garden school archivists knows all about run and fell seaming and gold thread embroidery? I didn't; I asked a technician. A what? A technician. It is time to explain.

It is a commonplace that any decent secondary school staff room can offer a range of knowledge and expertise that is far beyond the academic qualifications and professional experience of its inmates – because of the extent of their previous careers and leisure interests and pursuits. You can walk into any staff room and say, 'Does anyone know anything about?'… whatever it is, and the chances are that you will at once be regaled with willing, clear, succinct, comprehensive and well-informed advice.

All right, these people are in the knowledge business; you would expect that. Maybe. But what may come as a surprise is that, in a school like ours, there is another breed of people who can provide similar surprising ranges of knowledge. I come to the technicians.

Now, to most of us, a technician is a silent, shadowy individual in a white overall who drifts about laboratories, cupboards, preparation rooms, classrooms and demonstrations halls, setting up all kinds of complicated equipment. As a break from routine, he may occasionally twiddle a knob or two, or mend a broken tool.

He doesn't speak; he doesn't show any emotion; he doesn't do anything much except exchange mumbled monosyllables with the teacher before going off on yet another errand of mystery. He de-materialises at about four in the afternoon, and he re-appears at seven minutes to nine the next morning. If a pupil were to bump into him in the car park, he probably wouldn't recognise him without his white overall.

Take Alan Rogers, the Technician in the I.T. Department. OK, so he's your home-based computer boffin, the chap who comes to dig you out when your computer crashes, or to explain for the seventeenth time some routine piece of procedure to enable you to get into the programme you want before you wrench out the last of your hair.

But just look at what Alan knows. He knows about machine shop practice, drawing office practice, about digital and analogue control systems, about electronic testing and quality control. He is an electronics engineer, naturally, and has been a designer, manufacturer, manager and consultant. He has also run his own business, which has taken him into every conceivable aspect – creation, development, production, marketing and after-sales service. I am picking out things at random; I could quote a lot more. And this man is, officially, a 'Technician'. He is now, to be strictly accurate, a 'Systems Manager', but the point I am making is still valid; he is one of those silent experts on whom academic staff depend.

Over the way, in the Physics Department, is David Price. David has served nearly sixteen years with the R.A.F. He knows all about, for example, hydraulic, pneumatic, fuel and oil systems; mechanical and electro/mechanical control systems; transmissions, drive trains and gas turbine engines. He knows how to maintain and service Hawk fighter/trainer aeroplanes, and two or three different types of helicopter. Much of this work, naturally, involved moving very heavy weights; David knows about inspecting, testing and repairing lifting equipment, and has also instructed and examined apprentices in this field. He has served in Northern Ireland and the Gulf War. He is computer literate (naturally), and is experienced in Windows, spreadsheets and word processors. Not content with his service qualifications and his two technical diplomas, he is currently studying for a B.Sc.

degree in mathematics and science with the Open University. Another 'Technician'.

Now – did I ask one of these very knowledgeable gentlemen about run and fell seaming or gold thread embroidery? No. But I would wager, if I had, either David or Alan could have tapped the Internet and come up with an answer or two. Besides being very knowledgeable, they are also very willing and helpful.

No. I asked Matthew Greer. Matthew is the part-time technician in the Art Department. Ah – the one who puts out the easels and sharpens the pencils? Hardly.

Matthew holds two academic qualifications – from Plymouth College of Art and Design and Central St Martin's School for Art and Design. He has worked for English National Opera; he has been a lecturer in a school of Art and Design. He has experience of organisation, design, cutting, in fact nearly every feature to do with the presentation of fashion shows. He has worked in England, France and America. He has experience of several media of communication, including television and film. More recently he has done a lot of freelance work, and has two or three totally independent and original fashion collections to his credit.

A 'Technician'.

All this expertise and knowledge, and a lot more, is available to the pupils of this School, in areas where the average pupil (and, quite possibly, many a teacher) would not suspect it. I have barely scratched the surface; there are a lot more 'Technicians' and 'General Assistants' knocking about. They generally mind their own business, and do their job with no fuss. But the reserves that are there!

I began by saying that any old blazer is not necessarily any old blazer, if you have the wit and the willingness to look. And a technician is a great deal more than a switch-twiddler, if you keep your eyes and your ears open. The riches run deep.

Building the Gymnasium.

Building sixth form accommodation above the quad.

Memorial Hall, 'new' labs. and gym. complete.

An aerial view taken before the Sixth Form Centre appeared. An eagle-eyed enthusiast might be able to place the year more accurately from the car parked at the front door.

Courtenay House, 1987. The teachers seated are, left to right: Mervyn Reilly, Robert Moor, John Whitfield, David Clark, [pupil], Tim Hall, Richard Carter, Tony Evans.

Teachers are not stuffy all the time. Chris Ponder enjoys nothing better than a spell of therapeutical medication in the stocks.

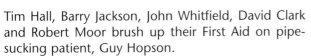

Tim Hall, Barry Jackson, John Whitfield, David Clark and Robert Moor brush up their First Aid on pipe-sucking patient, Guy Hopson.

STRONG AS LIONS

A lot of criticisms have been levelled at West Buckland School, and its inhabitants, over the years, as one might expect – by irate villagers, exasperated local farmers, rival academies, defeated sporting opponents, ill-disposed gossips, sceptical inspectors, shocked readers of graffiti on the backs of local church pews, patronising *blasé* visitors, doctrinaire opponents of private education, early leavers who couldn't play games, sufferers of stitch in Exmoor runs, survivors of exposure in the dormitories, baffled auditors, wary prospective parents (who changed their minds at the last minute) and nit-pickers in general.

But, after sifting through archive material for nearly two years, I am bound to conclude that there is one thing for which the School has never been criticised – its health. If ever there was a bunch of rude, vigorous, lusty lads (and, much later, lasses too), glowing with *bien-être*, it was, and is, the inmates of this remote moorland, stone-built, windswept, rain-soaked collection of gaunt classrooms and chilly passages, albeit now encrusted with a motley array of newer buildings. If one can imagine a hybrid of Greyfriars, Wuthering Heights, a brick-and-concrete council estate, and the Ideal Homes Exhibition, this is it.

This robust health was especially remarkable in the School's early days. In the mid-nineteenth century, mushrooming industrial cities, with their cramped, unplanned, streets, their poky, gloomy courtyards, their open sewers and diseased wells, were carrying off tens of thousands of poor wretches every year with cholera, typhus and pneumonia. Overworked doctors, without adequate funds, medicines and drugs, were powerless to prevent thousands more dying from smallpox, diphtheria, scarlet fever and malnutrition. The Prince Consort himself died of typhoid fever. In the very year of the School's foundation, 1858, occurred in London what became known as 'The Great Stink', when the Thames ran low during a very hot summer, and the raw sewage of two million inhabitants, which nearly strangled it, sent up a stench which came close to stifling the whole city. Parliament's windows were draped with curtains soaked in chloride of lime; Disraeli and Gladstone were both taken ill in the House because of the appalling atmosphere.

Forty years later, the Government was shocked by the large number of Army volunteers for campaigns like the Boer War who had to be rejected for being below the minimum level of health and fitness. It is no coincidence that within a few years laws had been passed about medical inspections and meals in schools.

This argument may be challenged – thus: it may be all very true, but it applied only in the cities, where public health was truly awful. West Buckland Farm and County School was in the depths of the country, and, as everyone knows, the country is much healthier than the city.

Not necessarily so. Rural families were not apple-cheeked, jolly souls who lived on roast beef and fruit pies and cream and good old English ale all the time. They were poor, most of them. Read *Lark Rise* by Flora Thompson, or the Revd Francis Kilvert's *Diary*. In the Great Agricultural Depression they got even poorer. A lot of the best produce was taken away on the new railways to feed the huge cities (or at least the inhabitants who could afford it). Children caught diseases in the country too, and died. If doctors were thin on the ground in cities, they were even thinner on the ground in the countryside. If running water and mains sewerage were slow in coming to the cities, they were slower still in coming to the villages. Add in a hefty dose of rural ignorance, a dollop of bovine conservatism, and garnish with old wives' tales and superstition – and you have a recipe for anything but glowing health.

All of which therefore makes the record of the School, especially in its early days, that much more creditable. As Jon Edmunds has said, 'we must distinguish between medical treatment and medical care'. It would appear that the School did look after its pupils very well – by the standards of the time. There were the usual exhortations to parents to notify the School of any exposure to infectious disease during the holidays. The School prospectuses nearly all mentioned a Matron, though it was not always clear whether her duties were primarily about clothes and bedding or about pills and bandages. Later on there was usually a Nursing Sister in attendance. From the days of the first permanent building, there was an infirmary, separate from the main block, for the care of patients with infectious diseases. The School grew a lot of its own vegetables and fruit. Remember its early pioneering idea of having a Farm School which might one day become self-sufficient. The fourth Headmaster, Mr Challen, made reference in 1896 to a School Laundry, 'for the exclusive use of the School'. Two years later, he added the further assurance that 'the possibility of infection is avoided'. He had second thoughts about this rash promise, and there is in the margin a pencilled note to insert 'risk' for 'possibility'. But the general optimism is undeniably there.

So it is hardly surprising that Headmasters were proud of the School's record. 'The health of the School has been wonderfully good' (Knight – H.M.'s Report for 1900-01). 'Remarkably good' (Badger). 'Remarkably good health record' (Westall). Challen noted that the School site was 'remarkable for its extreme healthiness'. Harries claimed that 'West Buckland boys are on the whole noted for their physique'. (We presume he meant 'healthy physique'.) In his final report, in the year he retired in 1934, Harries could assert that 'with the exception of a few cases of chicken pox in the Lent Term, the School has once more maintained its reputation for good health'.

Knight was moved to go further. In his report for 1906, he said, 'The health of the boys has been remarkably good; indeed, I do not think any School could produce a cleaner bill of health than the Devon County School. This ought to be a strong recommendation to parents.' (Indeed it ought, and it was no doubt intended to be.)

It would be tempting to dismiss the occasional remark like this as the predictable high gloss that any headmaster would put on his school in order to attract customers. But it happens so many times that the interpretation finally occurs to the reader that the claim may in fact be none other than true. This is reinforced by external, independent evidence as well. There was an article in *The Globe* for 13 November 1875, which mentioned 'a detached sick room, standing off some 70 yards from the main building, for cases of infectious disease. For the past five years, however, no use has been found for this establishment. The School would appear indeed to be especially healthy.' So outside observers found themselves falling into the same superlatives.

The Medical Officer's Report of 1935 found 'a high level of physical fitness, good nutrition and personal cleanliness'. It even went so far as to say that the boarders' personal cleanliness was better than that of the day boys – which is another feather in a boarding school's cap.

Was school health therefore perfect? No, of course not. Were there no epidemics? Yes, there were. But not many. Certainly, it would appear, considerably fewer than the national average.

There was a local epidemic referred to in 1935, which kept the pupils confined to barracks. We don't know if any germs actually seeped in from the village. There was a case of scarlet fever as late as 1947 – as if the School did not have enough on its plate with the awesome winter of that year. There were the normal outbreaks of measles. The great post-war 'flu' epidemics of 1919 and 1949 might have taken their toll, but I have found no reference to them.

The worst, by far, that I have found evidence of was the great epidemic of scarlet fever of 1864, when it was

decided to evacuate the entire School in order to clear the buildings for cleansing and disinfecting. A fine record of this has been left for us by the Revd J.F. Chanter of Lynton, who was a pupil at the time.

It is a classic instance of how a situation that would cause an adult to wring his hands provides endless joy of discovery for a small boy. The School was divided into two – the older boys were sent to Hunter's Inn, at Heddon's Mouth, and the younger ones to Breadwick, at Kentisbury. As luck would have it, the young Chanter was sent by mistake to the older boys' accommodation at Hunter's Inn. There was a lengthy time lag while arrangements were made to transport this small displaced person to Kentisbury, 6 miles away.

He was too young to take part in the senior lessons. It was summer time. He had all day on his hands. And the Devil made plenty of work for this resilient junior who was later to become a man of the cloth. He made the acquaintance of the most undesirable woman in the area – Patsy Geen, a witch it was said, and related to a family of sheep-stealers. He went fishing for congers with Widden the blacksmith, and ate Mrs Widden's conger eel pies. He got the local carpenter to make a boat for him, and sailed in it at the river's mouth. He risked his neck having races down the near-precipitous, scree-covered sides of hills. He went to a harvest home, and tasted ancient delights like frumenty, junket and metheglin.

In his account of this unforgettable summer, the Revd Chanter, obviously with great relish, offered tantalising hints of further escapades – like the theft of old Mrs Norman's crutches, the setting fire to the woods, and – best of all – taking out the weight and pendulum of the miller's grandfather clock, hiding inside the clock case, and making weird noises which frightened the miller's children half to death. As the years went by, he must have chortled behind his dog-collar many times as he relived this arcadian, halcyon summer for the benefit of his children and his choir-boys, and no doubt the stories grew a little taller with each telling.

However, to return to the main theme, it would seem that, when all was said and done, the School did indeed have a pretty good health record. Which brings us to the inevitable question – how did they do it?

The School was not rich; far from it. It could not pay for expensive fittings and comforts. It had no mains water; it depended on springs and wells, later reservoirs. Harries proudly proclaimed that the changing rooms were 'heated by hot water', carefully omitting to say that the dormitories were not. Hot baths were available – once a week, he said. He generously pointed out that boys, if they wished, could have a cold bath every morning 'by permission'.

Electricity came late. Gas even later. Outside toilets persisted for years. Central heating did not reach the dormitories till the nineteen-seventies, never mind the eighteen-seventies (and the boys were not overjoyed at its arrival, according to the Clothing Matron of the time). Governors' Minutes are full of references to cesspits and septic tanks. On the face of it, with all those wild rodents within a stone's throw out in the surrounding fields, it would seem a wonder that the School escaped the Black Death, never mind the measles.

Clearly it could not be put down solely to all those conscientious parents who dutifully wrote to inform the Headmaster that their son had been playing games with the boy next door who had had mumps.

So – why was the School so dashed fit?

I have never come across any medical authority who has said that fresh air is bad for you, and fresh air is a commodity that is in plentiful supply at West Buckland. Ask anybody who has spent more than ten minutes there. It is 650 feet above sea level, and swept by more winds than the Eddystone Light. All passages, archways and covered walks are specially designed so as to funnel them with greater sharpness and malice to other parts of the School. Mercury in the thermometers seems to be that much heavier than in thermometers elsewhere in North Devon, because it has such trouble creeping up the tube. Rain, by some law of meteorological geometry, comes in more horizontal than it does in, say, Barnstaple or South Molton.

I think, then, we have established to the satisfaction of the court that fresh air is a significant feature of life at West Buckland. 'Bracing' is an epithet which comes readily to mind.

'Remote' is another. West Buckland is well away from the germs of the towns and the markets. More to the point, until relatively recently, the vast majority of the pupils were boarders; there were few outsiders to bring in germs from the surrounding population. Pupils as late as the nineteen-sixties were allowed out to town only twice a term. Staff, certainly until school-teachers could as a matter of course own motor cars, mostly lived in. In short, nobody went anywhere much, and nobody came in much either.

So their health was in a kind of way ready-made for them. We presume that the vast majority of new pupils were of sufficient strength and resilience to be in a position for their parents to consider sending them in the first place. One School prospectus from about the nineteen-fifties or -sixties was careful to point out that 'boys suffering from weakness of bladder or sleepwalking, and delicate boys needing constant care and attention or special diets cannot be accepted'. It sounded a bit like the Foreign Legion.

The boys who arrived, and their teachers who received them, then put their minds to work to 'make' their health too. The West Buckland ethos of games and outdoor activities was not born by accident. True, cricket and football came naturally, as they would have done anywhere in mid-Victorian England. But how many other schools would have got around to holding an annual event which demanded that all able-bodied pupils over a certain age should cover over sixteen miles, up hill and down dale, in a competitive manner? In the twentieth century, it was not entirely unexpected that the School, with Exmoor on its doorstep and huge waves tumbling into Croyde Bay, should encourage walking, camping, rock climbing and surfing – which cater for the individual as well as the sacred team.

But as early as 1900, the authorities were becoming aware that it was not a good idea to foster the image of West Buckland as a place where the boys did nothing but study and pound round a field or a moor. Mr Knight, for example, well understood that not every boy was suited to ball games, but was equally aware that if they were healthy they still needed to be kept occupied. As he shrewdly observed in one of his reports, 'Healthy, vigorous boys do not do nothing.' Moreover, he was smarting from an observation in a recent Inspectors' Report: 'The life of the School seemed to be entirely confined to work and games.'

So the School endeavoured to improve matters with a Reading Room, a Manual Workshop, a Reading and Debating Society (ancestor of the Phoenix), and so on. Trying to strike a balance – the key to mental health, which in turn is the key to bodily health. Lord Fortescue, in a speech at Prize Day in 1871, had, long before, hoped that 'the countenances and appearance of the boys in this School would satisfy both parents and visitors that health was not sacrificed to study'.

Well, maybe so. Whatever were the results, you have to admit that the School authorities did try. They really did.

Nowhere more so than with the business of water. They must have cottoned on very early to the basic truth which the Water Rat expressed so feelingly: 'there is nothing – absolutely nothing – half so much worth doing as simply messing about in boats.' Well, they didn't have the boats, but they set about the business of providing the water as soon as they could.

Interestingly, and as if to prove the truth of the Water Rat's philosophy, the boys beat them to it. Three boys from Bishop's Tawton were the first pupils of the 'West Buckland Farm and County School' in 1858. The longest surviving one, Henry Tyte, wrote some reminiscences in the *Register* of nearly fifty years later. In them he gives an account of a pond that the boys made themselves, by damming up a small river, in the summer of 1859. They were, he said, 'greatly in need of a bathing pond'. Notice the word 'need'. It was not simply 'nice', or 'fun'; they 'needed' it.

Within a decade of the opening of the permanent building in 1861, the School authorities lent their own weight to the construction of a bathing pond in the School grounds. The *Register* recorded its opening in 1869, and even recorded the name of the first bather – 'W. Cade'. As the date was Saturday, 16 April, one can only admire the fortitude and hardiness of Master Cade.

The 'pond' was considered of sufficient importance to the well-being of the pupils to be worth mentioning in nearly every prospectus surviving from the late nineteenth century. In 1881, for instance, parents were not only told of a 'large bathing pond' where 'most of the boys learn to swim', but were told of its cost – 'about £150'.

The new Headmaster, Mr Bland, no doubt in an effort to raise the profile of the School, referred to it in 1889 as a 'swimming-bath'. His successor, Mr Challen, who believed in calling a spade a spade, reverted to the original nomenclature of 'pond', but restored the 'large'.

Early *Register* editions referred to races in the pond – up and down, twice each way. What must it have been like? What were the surroundings? Bullrushes and concrete? Algae and furtive cigarette papers? Jagged corners and grazed knees? Bird droppings and cow pats? How compulsory was swimming? What really went on? Secret picnics and sunbathing? Unofficial dumping of bad reports which must not reach the eyes of parents? Blessed peace for the rare sensitive boy who craved an oasis of solitude away from the relentless hearty party of the jolly old team? Did 'most of the boys' really 'learn to swim'? We have next to no evidence.

We do, however, have one or two photographs of the new pool, which was completed in about 1905, at a cost of £198.10s – not all that much more than the original pond. The *Register* published a complete account of costs and subscriptions – there was a short-fall of £64.19s.1d. Sizeable too – Harries in one of his prospectuses gave the measurements – 60 feet by 30, and made of concrete.

The School, as early as 1905, had evolved its instinct for thrift, and used the timber which it had employed as moulds for the concrete to build a new cricket pavilion. (The old one had been blown down by a gale in September 1903.)

The surviving photos show the usual gaggle of boys disporting themselves, with the shots from the prospectuses carefully indicating the presence of a member of staff. There was one quaint feature to show that boys as well as girls could become victims of the Great Dictator – Fashion: where the swimming costumes from between the wars were full – that is, they had a 'vest' part – some young bloods sported an off-the-shoulder style for one of the straps. My dear!

– the 'in' thing. I have also been assured, though I have seen no documentary evidence of it, that at one period boys were not required to wear a swimming costume at all; indeed, one version of this legend claims that they were forbidden.

So – fresh air, bracing sports, long runs, cold baths, early spring and late autumn dips, nude or otherwise – a truly Spartan regime. And it seemed to work.

Tom Hitchins, whose memories are recorded elsewhere in this work, says that he never had a single day in sick bay in all the time he was at the School. I have no doubt that there are plenty of other Old Boys who can claim the same. From the earliest days of the cadet camps at Aldershot, the stories grew about the contingent from West Buckland School: they may have been a bit rough round the edges, but they took in their stride every hardship and every stern test that the Army authorities placed before them – and better than many of the cadets from the more fashionable establishments. There is ample testimony moreover, from Old Boys who survived war and prison camp, that the experience gained at W.B. stood them in very good stead.

What would they all make of it now? Now that the School has a covered pool, central heating, hot showers and baths (and not just once a week), inside toilets, recreation rooms, covered walkways, doctors, dentists, educational psychologists, house parents, counsellors, private motor cars for Sixth Formers, air-conditioned coaches for nearly everyone else, hundreds of day pupils, hundreds of girls, discos, parties, barbecues, computer games, snooker tables, mobile 'phones, alternative vegetarian menus, and so on and so on.

They may indeed shake their grey heads and say that things are not what they used to be.

True. But look at these kids today. Do they strike you as any less healthy than their predecessors? Can we criticise them for being not like their predecessors, when they play so many games, walk the Ten Tors, achieve Duke of Edinburgh's gold medals, take 'years out' all over the globe, carry off awards for Young Enterprise, collect pilot's licences, raise money with sponsored walking and running, sponsored fencing, sponsored swims, reads, silences, and sponsored goodness knows what else?

If they are just as robust, do we look elsewhere for reasons? Or is it still the fresh air and the long runs? And the water?

'The Exmoor' Run

A good illustration of just how isolated the School was, and is. To think of putting a school here at all was in itself a feat of imagination and optimism.

From the *Register* of June, 1910. So things haven't changed much.

Briefing in the rain. It looks as if the boy at the left of the back row is wearing an old rugby colours cap.

Ready for the 'off' (probably 1920s).

Late 1920s, at a guess. Look at the cars. Mr Garfield Pearce, senior and L.V. Hudson.

A rare picture of Mrs Harries. Mr Harries was much photographed, and his mother was in several staff photographs. But Harries' wife does not appear much.

The winner – in this case M. Tully, who won twice – in 1935 and 1936. He also won the Colts race twice, in 1930 and 1931, and the Junior 'Exmoor' twice, in 1932 and 1933, and came second in the main 'Exmoor' in 1934.

The only runner with a better record is J.R. Jones, who won the 'Exmoor' four times – 1954-57 – and in the same years won both Half-Mile and Mile races – four times. Postscript: Another Tully, also in Brereton, won the 'Exmoor' in 1968, though six minutes more slowly than (?) his father.

Another moment from between the wars.

A welcome end. The master with the pipe is 'Watto' – Mr Watson, music master. And it might be Sam Howells with him.

Waiting at the Poltimore Arms, 1962.

David Clark with the starters from his house, the Courtenay – March, 1980.

Paul Thornhill with some chilly but cheery competitors – March, 1979. This race began, not on Five Barrows, but outside the Poltimore Arms. Perhaps that explains why they were so cheery.

Before they thin out – 1979.

Two of the great accompaniments – mud and 'bovine residue' – Junior 'Exmoor', 1973.

A daunting prospect.

The latest trend in 'Exmoor' gear – fresh from the catwalk.

Snow forced the cancellation of only one Exmoor in 142 years – in 1947.

Building and using the pool, which opened in 1905

The pool in 1926. Despite the legend that there was a period when the boys swam nude, these pupils seem pretty comprehensively clad. There are one or two touches of revolt with the fetching off-the-shoulder style sported by some young bloods – one shoulder only, you understand. A bit like having the ring in the correct nostril.

At a guess, the fifties or sixties, possibly later. But apart from the fashions, nothing seems to have changed much.

Again, between the wars. Note the addition of a sort of spring board, albeit a low one, and the foreshortened diver in mid-air.

A typical team of beefy ruggernauts from 1936, by which time the game was just over a decade old at W.B. It is unlikely that you would see spectacles and moustaches in a school scrum these days; indeed it is increasingly unlikely that you would even see hair.

The last team photograph surviving showing the colours caps. Yet another casualty of the War.

Most rugby players at W.B. were, by definition, average. This, then, is more likely to be the recollection of most players – the elements.

Or this – on the rare fine days.

If the signatures on the back of this postcard can be deciphered reliably, they belong to Pryn, Hill, Morley Stephens, Bentall, Partridge, Pascoe, Webber, Hume, Brown, and (possibly) Hitchcock

The cricketers of 1963.

Not one of the commonest school extra-mural activities.

Derek Holt started the School fencing, and must be one of the few teachers who can claim to have produced an international in a 'new' sport – Charlotte Read, who won a gold medal at the Commonwealth Games at Kuala Lumpur.

Another 'new' sport – boys' hockey, with its prophet and inspiration, Richard Baker. Note the high proportion of Asian members. It faded for a while, and now is enjoying a comeback, thanks to Chris Burrows and Colin Gambles. Foreign tours have already taken place.

A typical group of intrepid Ten Tors expeditionists, from the 45-mile course of 1979.

A Lorry Load

A chance acquaintance on the island of Corsica led to the discovery of another West Buckland author besides R.F. Delderfield and Brian Aldiss. A teacher of French and Spanish in the School, Martine le Barth, was on holiday there when she met Robert Armstrong. It came out in their conversation that he had attended West Buckland between 1958 and 1965, and now lives in Aosta, in Italy. It came out too that he has published a book on Scammell heavy vehicles – a sumptuous volume with glorious illustrations and text in four languages.

Mr Armstrong was happy to donate a copy to the School Library, where it now resides very impressively – it weighs almost as much as the vehicles it celebrates.

Richard Carter, the Physics teacher, is the son and grandson of Old Members of the School. He also had three great-uncles and five cousins in the School. All four of his sons attended the School too, and, like him, all four went to Peterhouse College, Cambridge.

◙ FIRST LADY ◙

If you had asked an ill-disposed critic of West Buckland Old Boys' Association what was wrong with it, he might have said two things: it was too old and it had too many boys. Which, at first sight, seems a contradiction in terms. What is wrong with an Old Boys' Association having Old Boys in it?

To which, one might answer, 'Nothing, so long as they are Old Boys, and not all old boys.' It would be a safe bet, I venture to suggest, that if you asked a score of Old Boy committees up and down the country what their chief problem was, three-quarters of them would say 'attracting a younger membership'. Persuading the recent leavers to join. Or, if they have been automatically enrolled, persuading them to come to Old Boy functions. It is a problem to break down their reluctance to share social occasions, not with Old Boys, but with old boys.

Secondly, as co-education has spread among more and more schools, it may be an equal problem persuading old female pupils to come along to join the boys – whether old, Old, or young.

One remedy was to change the name of the organisation – to nail one's bisexual colours to the mast, as you might say. So the 'Old Boys' Association' has become the 'Old West Buckland Association', with no reference to sex at all.

But that was not enough. It was not enough to give the Old Girls a ride on the boat; sooner or later they would have to be given a chance to crew for it, and, in the end, steer it – skipper it. And that is what, in 1999 happened. Rachel Withecombe became the first female Old Member of the School to become the Association's President.

Rachel said she was flattered and honoured, and 'a little hesitant', but she knew that she was not without resources or experience. She had been involved in the Association almost since leaving school, and had served as Committee Member and as Vice-President. She was married to an Old Boy. She worked in the School, which gave her an insight denied to most other presidents. And she worked as a non-teacher. 'We see a different side.'

Her husband was already Treasurer. It was this, actually, which helped to cause her to be 'a little hesitant'; was it too much to have two key officials in the same family? But her misgivings must have been overcome, quite possibly by very senior members like Tom Hitchins, who, from his great vantage point of age, could see the benefits of reform more clearly perhaps than middle-aged men who had not reached the cavalier disdain for convention attained by the really old. Middle age brings experience and assurance, but it takes real age to bring wisdom.

It was certainly Tom, and another senior member, Dudley Swinney, who championed her candidature.

Obviously, she had youth on her side, as well as her sex. By simply being herself, she was an incentive to Old Girls to join – above all to young Old Girls. This was vindicated triumphantly at the recent London Dinner, when a record number of Old Girls attended. A second success has been to persuade another lady, and a young one, to join the Committee in the coming September.

Finally, her professional experience, as Nursing Sister, meant that she was going to be no shrinking violet. She proved well able to cope with the leg-pulling that any pioneer must expect. Curiously, she said, when she had first joined the Committee, they had behaved almost as if she didn't exist. Later, when she became President, the jokes and the remarks never strayed into the ghetto of bad taste. Indeed, she said, many members had been very helpful.

As the wife of a Committee Member, and as an ex-Committee Member herself, she knew exactly what she was letting herself in for, and the prospect did not appal her. She did admit to getting 'a little bit anxious before Committee meetings', because 'I'm not a natural'. But as a nurse, she was not afraid to tell people things they were not expecting, or were unwilling, to hear, and she was no doubt also good at wrapping up unpleasant truths when it became necessary.

There was plenty to do. Her predecessor, David Walker, had identified some fields in which there needed to be some significant advances – raising the O.W.B.A. profile generally, developing the Charitable Trust, building a working relationship with a new Headmaster, and so on.

There were the public functions – the dinners. 'I'm not a natural at public speaking.' She found the prospect 'very daunting'. But she took on board her husband's advice that you can't prepare enough, and, despite the fact that she admitted that she 'hardly heard what the other speakers before me were saying', she acquitted herself well. 'My friends, knowing me,… said, in effect, "Well done".'

Has the year had any regrets? Of course. It was a pity that the Summer Ball had to be scaled down. The O.W.B.A. profile could be improved through more publications. They are constantly looking for ways to give money to the School, without casting the Association in the role of corporate sugar daddy.

(They keep funds, she said, in deep investments. There was a strong tradition in the Association for bringing serious financial support to the School in times of crisis [as this book has, I hope, amply shown], and there was therefore an equally strong tradition of keeping something by for a rainy day.)

Has she noticed any other traditions? For instance, was there a 'typical' president? Had she tried to fit herself to that tradition? She would only go so far as to say that there have been some presidents who have been definitely more memorable than others. But no – 'I have tried to be myself.'

And that was the advice, she said, she would give to any other lady who took on the President's role. 'Just be yourself and make of it what you want it to be. Don't overstretch yourself. Remember it is not so much a position of power as a position of honour.' Like the Queen, I suggested, with only a hint of face-tiousness. As we both thought about it, we seemed, at the same moment, to agree that it was not so far out.

For a person who said she was 'not a natural', and who didn't think presidents should 'push themselves', she carried a pretty solid portfolio of ideas, aspirations and philosophies.

Yes, there should be more lady presidents, though only if suitable ones present themselves. It was not sensible to lay down set rules about regular alternations. It was far more important to alternate between young and old rather between male and female.

She valued particularly the contribution of many Old Boys' wives, and she looked forward to the day when they can be awarded honorary membership as a sign of gratitude for their work.

The Old Members' Association was there to offer support, not advice. The running of the School should be left to the professionals. But because it supported the School, the Association itself deserved support, because that was its sole raison d'être. Its sporting and social occasions were good fun, but the real and only reason for its existence was to support the School. 'I believe the O.W.B.A. is a good organisation, and it deserves to be taken seriously.'

Rachel had unquestionably enjoyed her year as President. She was proud of several things. Of her appointment, obviously. Of the many compliments she had received on her stewardship. She was touched by the number of her old fellow-pupils who had come to the Dinner, and by the willingness of Michael Downward, her ex-Headmaster, to be Guest Speaker.

Her most moving memory had been the Memorial Service on Armistice Day, when the names on the Roll of Honour were read out. 'It brings a lump to the throat just talking about it.'

She was deeply aware that, ultimately, the O.W.B.A. is not about Old Boys or Old Girls, or about old boys or old girls, but about new boys and new girls, the present pupils. Her own work and experience on the staff have given her an insight that previous presidents, for the most part, did not have, and this has clearly coloured her approach and her work. She knows that neither she, nor any other ex-pupil, would have joined the Association at all if they had not harboured some softer feelings about the place which had educated them. Channelling those softer feelings into something worthwhile for that place seems, to her, a noble enterprise.

'I wanted to thank the School. It did a lot for me.'

Rachel Withecombe, first Lady President of the O.W.B.A.

The earliest known picture of an Old Boys' gathering, 1880. The variety of headgear is extraordinary. One boy (left centre front) even sports a sailor cap like the Tsarevich. Who knows? – perhaps the naval traditions of English and Russian royal families made them fashionable.

A more formal group, from 1883. Because of the number of moustaches in the back row, and the sprinkling of cricket flannels, this was probably an Old Boys' gathering. It might be Thompson on the extreme left. It is certainly Mr Thomas, another master, on the extreme right.

The Old Boys' football eleven of 1898.
Rear: C. Wheeler [sub.] (1895-1902), Carter (G.N. – 1893-1897), L. Pollard (1883-85), A.G. Hind, Hawkins, R.G. Mothersdale (1892-95).
Front: P.C. Adams, A.J. Andrews, G.E. Mortimer (1891-96), J. Hall (? – 1896), J.F. Sanders (1890-92). The baby-faced substitute, Wheeler, was to become a Headmaster of the School, and the longest-serving Governor.
With the exception of Pollard, they were all pretty recent leavers.
And see how well polished their boots were.

The Old Boys' gathering, 1901. Standing: H. Pickard (1896-1901), J.R. Barber (1898-1904), W. Stradling (1890-98), E.C. Harries (master, 1900-04), H.T.H. Lancaster (1872-74), Comer Clarke (1870-76), R.H. Spear (master, 1900-03), R. Sanders (1897-1903), A.W. Rabley, W.O. Keats (1886-87).
Chairs: A. Taylor (master, 1895-1929), H.R. Champion (1888-93), H. Packer (1883-86), B. Spicer (1871-73), W.A. Knight (Headmaster, 1900-07), F.W. Taplin (1870-75), C. Wheeler (1895-1902).
Ground: R. Fordham (1899-1902), H.R. Davey (1899-1903), G.E.L. Carter (1896-1904), T.H. Watts (1897-1903), J.W. Carter .

This group of cricketers was bursting with talent. Barber later played for Middlesex, and was to become the captain of a team called – wait for it – the Crouch End Vampires. Stradling was probably the most talented all-rounder the School produced in its first fifty years, and mopped up prizes and distinctions in the classroom and on the games field. Among many other things, he captained St John's College, Cambridge at cricket. Harry Packer played rugby for Wales in the 1890s (see 'God for Harry, England, and St George'). Harries played cricket for Somerset. Fred Taplin was one of the famous six Taplin brothers who attended D.C.S. G.E.L. Carter set the trend for academic distinction in the Carter family which is continued at W.B. to this day; Richard Carter, the Physics teacher, attended Peterhouse College, Cambridge; so did all his four sons. From the front row, T.H. Watts, held the School record for throwing the cricket ball – 105 yards and 3 inches – which would take some beating today. He also went on to play football for Notts County. The massive figure in the centre, Spicer, was, according to a *Register* from 1907, 'Captain of Cambridge University Long Vacation Club'.

The Old Boys' Match, August, 1885.
Back: A.D. Thomas, H.J. Vine, W.H. Taplin, F.R. Hill, J. Carter, R.A.W. Barfoot, Mr. Thomas (master), J.G. Shain (master), L.R. Ashford, H.A. Vivian, H.L.Luxton, R.M. Latham (master).
Centre: F.O. Taylor, E.G. Taplin, E.T. Loram, F.W. Taplin, S.H. Tamlyn, H.H. Taplin.
Front: Comer Clarke, W.E. Calvert (master), F.A. Wells, W.H. Taplin, Revd J.H. Thompson (H.M.), T.R.Potbury, L.L. Taplin

Another Old Boys' team, from 1908.
Rear: C. Wheeler (this time present in his own right, as it were), A.J. Pike (1899-1903), M. Trump (1899), C.C. Youings (1898-99), R.C. Webb (1895-98), M.I. Shave (1901-03).
Front: C. Pearce (1900-03), R.H. Smyth (1895-98), E.G. Trump (1894-96), A.T. Saunder [the expected 's' at the end of the name is crossed out in the original] (1895-98), R. Sanders (1897-1903).
Note how short the average stay at the School was – a fact often deplored by the headmasters of the time.

The Old Boys' Dinner of 1912, in London. The Chairman, standing, is Harold Hilton, the golf international and Open Champion.

An austerity Old Boys' Dinner of 1947. It is a long way from the moustachioed opulence of the 1912 occasion.

❀ A WORM'S EYE VIEW ❀

On 24 June 2000, a new building was officially declared open. And named. The 'Delderfield' building.

Anyone who writes about West Buckland School has, sooner or later, to inform his readers that the novelist and playwright, R.F. Delderfield, was a pupil here. Sooner or later, too, he has to remark that R.F.D. made his literary fortune with a West End hit play called *Worm's Eye View*, and that he made the television hit charts with the dramatisation of his novel – about the School – called *To Serve Them All My Days*. R.F.D. wrote a lot of other stuff too – much of it well received and very successful – but it seems that posterity has decided that it is these two works which will encapsulate his memory in the mind of the general literary consumer. (Arthur Conan Doyle often bemoaned the fact that the public insisted on remembering him for Sherlock Holmes, when, in his own opinion, he had written a great deal of much more memorable material, but that was posterity's verdict, and there was not much he could do about it.)

Be that as it may, when the School authorities were casting about for a celebrity name to attach to the new block, Delderfield's was the one that floated to the surface.

So 'the Prep.' has a new home. (So does the I.T. Department upstairs, but it is the Prep. which is the subject of this piece, so the I.T. Department will, I'm afraid, have to wait for a while till we can get round to giving them the exclusive treatment and literary longevity they deserve.)

Its previous home was in a house called 'Langholme', from which it took its name. So 'the Prep.' is comparatively recent. Indeed, one would be forgiven for thinking that the whole concept of a preparatory school is comparatively recent. The earliest photograph I can find for it is dated 1970, and shows Charles Phelps in the middle of a well-scrubbed phalanx of juniors. The date – 1970 – may not be entirely unconnected with the desire of the Headmaster, the Revd George Ridding, to try, in a period of severe financial stringency, to generate a little more revenue.

Charles was succeeded by Malcolm Symonds, who sadly died in office. Laurence Whittal-Williams then took over, and shared the running of it with his wife Judith as house-mother. All this time it was a house, just another 'house' in the School.

Then it changed its status. Jon Edmunds was appointed to be a 'headmaster', not of a house, but of a separate sort of school, though it was still called 'Langholme'. He left in about 1990 to become the head of a choir school in Oxford, and was succeeded by Gary Benfield. When Gary left, the status of the school was changed again, and it became incorporated in the main body of the School once more, though its principal teacher, now Andrew Moore, retains the 'rank' of Headmaster. It now has 150 pupils.

So much for the bread-and-butter history of it.

Of more interest, I hope, to the reader is the fact that 'the Prep.' is nothing new. (Trust a historian to tell you that.) It is not new now; it was not new when Jon Edmunds came to be the head of a new 'school'. It was not even new when Charles Phelps started it up in a nearby house called 'Langholme'.

It goes right back to the very beginnings of the 'West Buckland Farm and County School' – right back to 1859 – right back to within three months of the very first beginnings in the much-recorded farmhouse at Stoodleigh in November 1858. There is in the Archive a printed prospectus from that same West Buckland Farm and County School, which informs its (anticipated) many readers that 'it is proposed to establish, in connection with this School, a PREPARATORY SCHOOL for younger boys, who will not work on the Farm, but will receive a thoroughly good Elementary Education preparatory to their entering the Upper School'.

The Lower School would have its own 'efficient' master, 'with whom the Boys may board and lodge, but will be under the immediate superintendence of the Master of the Upper School'. There it is again – the idea of separation, but pretty strict surveillance at the same time.

The fees were going to be 'four guineas per quarter', but day boys would pay only one guinea a quarter. (A guinea was equivalent to £1.05p., so the fees amounted to £16.20 a year.) There were to be 'no extras'. Even allowing for inflation since 1859, this should strike the reader as pretty reasonable, and it was intended to be; remember the founders' oft-repeated claim that they were trying to establish a system of education for 'the middle classes'.

This school would open, it said, 'about the 20th January'. The year is not given, but it must be 1859, because a later printed prospectus, which is dated – 1 August 1859 – states that of the 33 pupils currently in the School, 17 belonged 'to the Preparatory Division'. Indeed the School was practically full, because the prospectus also said that 'no more Boarders can be received at present'. Parents who wished to board their sons were requested to tell the Headmaster 'at Michaelmas', 'in order that additional accommodation may be provided'. So the School was doing well in its first year, and the response that Brereton had predicted and hoped for was clearly there – in all age groups.

There was one difference between the 'Preparatory Division' then and 'the Prep.' now: nowadays the change-over takes place at eleven; in 1859, Thompson, the first Headmaster, explained to parents and well-wishers at one of the first public meetings they had that the cut-off age was thirteen. Curiously parallel to the system that pertains today in many more fashionable 'preps.' which serve the top league of public schools.

By the late 1860s, the prospectus is boasting that the School roll has gone up to nearly 100, but one has to wait till the last page to find a reference to those pupils under thirteen, who get charged two guineas a year less than their elders. The division between under thirteen and over thirteen persisted throughout Thompson's Headship – till 1888, that is – but one wonders how many of those juniors were under the age of eleven.

One wonders because, from the 1870s onward, Thompson used to attend regular conferences of county school headmasters. Devon County School was the first such school, but others soon grew up, and are now well-established public schools – like Cranleigh, Hurstpierpoint, Ardingly, Framlingham, Whitgift, City of London, and so on. At these conferences, the assembled heads would complain that they found it difficult to maintain standards because the calibre of pupil sent to them by the feeder primary schools was too random and inconsistent. If they were taking in a lot of younger pupils themselves, surely they would not have been complaining so much. So one is left with the conclusion that most parents were not making the sacrifice of fees until their sons had passed the age of ten, or eleven, or more. No registers survive from this period, no record of individual pupils' ages.

The next Headmaster, Bland, kept up the over-thirteen/under-thirteen division. So did his successor, Challen. And not much evidence appears to suggest that any special provision was being made for the lower half. One of Challen's later prospectuses says that 'the general course of studies is such as to fit pupils for Mercantile or Agricultural pursuits, or for a Professional career.' But the School is already raising its sights, already trying to gain its place among the more long-standing establishments. The prospectus also says, in the very next sentence, 'Boys are besides specially prepared for the Universities, the Civil Service, and for the different Public Examinations.' Moving away from that 'middle-class education' for the sons of local farmers and tradesmen.

Challen went on to say that every boy, right down to the Third Form, would be 'required to enter each year for the Cambridge Local Examinations'. 'The two Lower Forms (i.e. II and I) are examined by the masters.' (This is the only specific reference to the younger members of the School, apart from the obvious mention of Reading, Writing, Spelling, Grammar and 'the Scriptures', which no doubt everybody did anyway.) But we still don't know how young these boys were.

The only hint of the presence of small boys comes from an explanation of the School's very idiosyncratic version of 'Foot-ball', which placed no limit on the number of players in a game. It was pointed out that in the interests of safety, it was not wise to allow the smallest boys to participate (if indeed the poor terrified pups would have wanted to), but once again we don't know the actual age of these 'youngest boys'.

The first clear indication of the School's interest in those of a modern 'Prep.' age comes in a prospectus of Mr Knight, who was Headmaster from 1900 to 1907. 'Boys,' said Mr Knight, 'can enter at eight years of age.'

There are probably two reasons for this. First, when Knight took over, after his predecessor Challen had departed taking two-thirds of the pupils with him, the school roll stood, at its lowest, at 31. The School had boarding accommodation for well over 100. So Knight badly needed boys at desks and bodies in beds.

Secondly, Knight complained in one of his H.M.'s reports that it was a shame that boys did not stay very long at the School. The average stay was under two years. Jon Edmunds, in his history of the School, gives similar figures; in the first six or eight years of Harries' rule, the average time had barely reached three years, and between 1907 and 1914, only six boys out of 225 who left the School in that period had stayed for the full seven years.

So – the philosophy clearly became, quite simply, 'catch 'em young'. Knight also offered a financial inducement. Although there was still the difference between the costs of boys over thirteen (11 guineas a term) and those under thirteen (10 guineas a term), 'the lower fees are charged throughout their stay at the School for Boys who are admitted under the age of twelve'. Boys could also be admitted 'at any time during the Term, and a proportionate reduction in the Fees in such cases is allowed'.

Harries, who was appointed in 1907, continued the assault on parents of young children. 'A boy can enter the School at eight years of age, and parents are strongly urged to send boys at any rate before the age of twelve, so as to enable them to take full advantage of the systematic teaching of the Upper School, and to avoid the loss of time and energy often involved, at a critical period of a boy's life, by a change of schools.'

It worked. The numbers went up. No doubt there were other contributory factors – the new laboratories opened in 1904, the appointing of new staff – including ladies, the relief after the awful years of war, the boom years of the 1920s, the tremendous energy and drive of the Headmaster. Whatever the reasons, the school roll stood at 67 when Harries was appointed. By 1921 it stood at 200. True, it did go down again towards the end of his Headship, but that was not Harries' fault; that was the fault of the Great Depression.

Indeed, it worked so well that it would appear that the great drive to 'catch 'em young' eased up. The first surviving prospectus after 1908 – that of 1920 – makes no mention of the 'under-thirteen/over-thirteen' division. The only division now in fees is between 'boarders and day boys' – and there was no doubt about which of the two Harries preferred.

The 1920 prospectus makes no mention of a minimum entry age at all. So we are left to conclude that they didn't need the very young ones all that much.

This trend is continued in Westall's prospectuses. Moreover, the emphasis now seems to have shifted to the other end of the School – to the upper age brackets. 'Parents are urged to give their children two years in Form VI after they have gained their School Certificate [the equivalent of G.C.S.E.].' This tallies with the gradual orientation of the School towards the rest of the public schools. The School is now trying to play more games; it has switched to the more fashionable rugger from proletarian soccer; the old 'dormitories' are now called 'houses'; it is going after university distinction. It has long since dropped its 'County School' name and adopted another – just like Cranleigh and Framlingham and the rest.

By the nineteen-forties, Howells, the Head appointed in 1941, has come right out into the open and declared that 'the School accommodates 160 boarders (11-18)'. So there it is – no Prep. Stephens says it even more explicitly: 'Boys may enter from the age of ten, provided they pass the Entrance Examination… which is held for boys of about ten and eleven in March of each year for entry in the following September.' The eleven plus, in effect.

It is left, then, to George Ridding, appointed in 1968, to reverse the trend. A surviving prospectus from his rule specifically mentions a separate 'Preparatory Department', with, incidentally, fees which are only marginally lower than those of the main School – £462 per term as against £486. So 'the Prep.' was once again in business.

As with Knight and Harries at the beginning of the century, the conclusion seems inescapable that the incentive was the need for more income, more bodies at desks and in beds. When numbers were reliable, the drive for younger pupils fell off.

Now the wheel has come full circle. Indeed, it has come more than full circle. Over the last decade or so, the drive for younger and younger pupils has reached down to a sort of 'pre-Prep.' age. Most recently of all, a Nursery Department has opened. So in theory the School can now offer a continuous education to a pupil from the age of three to the age of eighteen – practically toilet-training to Oxbridge Entrance, from tying shoe laces to the Differential Calculus, from musical chairs to the Assault Course, from forward rolls to the Duke of Edinburgh's Gold Medal.

If firm bonds are forged during a pupil's secondary education here, from eleven to eighteen – and they often are – just think what sort of link can be fashioned during a possible stay of fifteen years. The potential is there for giving a child a temperamental rock of truly awesome stability – though at the same time it imposes on the School an equally awesome responsibility to make sure they get it right.

But it must seem a long way to go for little goblins of three and four as they wend their way, in lines, two by two, hand in hand, about the campus, gazing at all those anonymous kneecaps. It must indeed be a 'Worm's Eye View'. We can only hope that R.F.D. would have approved.

R.F. Delderfield, dramatist and novelist, author of *To Serve Them All My Days*, known to his contemporaries at W.B. as 'Dido'.

WEST BUCKLAND
FARM & COUNTY SCHOOL.

It is proposed to establish, in connection with this School, a

PREPARATORY SCHOOL

For younger Boys, who will not work on the Farm, but will receive a thoroughly good Elementary Education preparatory to their entering the Upper School.

This Lower School will be placed under an efficient Master, with whom the Boys may board and lodge, but will be under the immediate superintendence of the Master of the Upper School.

This School will open about the 20th January.

TERMS :

Boarders - - - Four Guineas per Quarter.
Day Boys - - - One Guinea   ,,
No Extras.

Parents are requested to communicate with Mr. THOMPSON, the Head Master.

The very first 'Prep.' prospectus, from 1859.

The first 'Prep.' photograph, from 1970. Charles Phelps is in the centre. On the left as you view, Malcolm and Norman Symms.

Devon County School,
WEST BUCKLAND.

WEDNESDAY Evening, October 18th, 1876.

A VERY SERIOUS AFFAIR.

Mr. Muffy ..	..(A Man of courage)	.. W. E. Calvert.
Mr. Theophilus	..(A courageous Man)	.. J. G. Shain.
George..	..	.. G. T. Llewellin.
Mrs. Muffy	..	.. W. H. Trounson.
Caroline	..(Mr. Muffy's Daughter)	.. T. Seldon.
Milkmaid	..	.. H. E. Leman.
Boy	..	.. R. R. Luxton.

FORTUNE'S FROLIC.

Robin Roughhead ..	(A Ploughman)..	.. J. G. Shain.
Mr. Snacks	(A Steward)	.. P. B. Riky.
Mr. Frank	(A reduced Gentleman)	.. W. E. Calvert.
Rattle	(A Banker's Clerk)	.. G. T. Llewellin.
Countryman	..	.. C. B. Meller.
James	..	.. R. R. Luxton.
Miss Nancy	(Snacks's Daughter)	.. F. A. Wells.
Dame Margery	..	.. W. H. Trounson.
Dolly	(Her Daughter)	.. T. Seldon.

GOODY TWO SHOES.

Marorry ..	(Goody Two Shoes)	.. F. W. Petter.
Ben Bobstay	(Her Brother)	.. R. Howell.
Christopher Clump	(A Cobbler)	.. C. B. Meller.
The Virtuous Squire	..	.. J. G. Shain.
Dame Tabitha Tickler	(The Village Schoolmistress)	W. H. Gribble.
Tom	(A Pupil at the Village School)	F. K. Brodie.
Dick	(Ditto)	.. R. R. Luxton.
Harry	(Ditto)	.. J. H. Harris.
Other Pupils at the Village School	..	{ R. Q. Harris. H. E. Leman.

To commence at Half-past Seven.

T. Hearson, Printer.

Devon County School,
WEST BUCKLAND.

MONDAY Evening, July 25th, 1881.

SHYLOCK,
OR
THE MERCHANT OF VENICE.

Shylock	..	.. R. P. Chope.
The Duke	..	.. F. H. White.
Antonio	..	.. A. E. P. Hughes.
Bassanio	..	.. L. T. Oakley.
Gratiano	..	.. C. S. Watson.
Salerio	..	.. A. E. Butt.
Clerk	..	.. F. A. Coon.
Portia	..	.. E. W. Gifford.
Nerissa	..	.. R. S. Harper.

A PHENOMENON IN A SMOCK FROCK.

Mr. Sowerberry	..	.. A. E. P. Hughes.
John Buttercup (a Milkman)	..	.. R. P. Chope.
Mr. Barker..	..	.. C. S. Watson.
James (Sowerberry's Servant)	..	.. L. T. Oakley.
Mrs. Barker	..	.. R. S. Harper.
Betsey Chirrup (Sowerberry's Housekeeper)	..	A. E. Butt.

To commence at Half-past Seven.

Devon County School.
West Buckland.
February 22nd, 1887.
To commence at 7.30 p.m.

Part I.

Pianoforte Solo	Feen Reigen (Reissiger)	W. Thomas.
Part Song	The Cuckoo sings in the poplar-tree (McFarren)	} The Choir.
Song	The Grasp of an English Hand	Rev. J. A. Thompson.
Glee	Dickory Dickory Dock (Allen)	The Choir.
Song	Thirty Years Ago	Rev. J. A. Thompson.
Glee	Sweet and Low (Barnby)	The Choir.
Reading	The News Boy's Debt	Rev. J. A. Thompson.
Song	A Boatman's Life for Me (&c.)	A. & S. Campbell.
Chorus	Swinging Valse (Silva)	The Choir.
Song	The Amateur Yachtsman (Law)	W. Thomas.
Singing Quadrilles on Nursery Rhymes (Snorer)		The Choir.
Reading	The Cocoanut man's Story	Rev. J. A. Thompson.

Part II.
I've Eaten my Friend.

Cockles (Proprietor of the Original Veal and Ham Pie Shop)		A. C. Curtis.
Wigsby (Proprietor of the Easy Shaving Shop)		H. S. Polberry.
Hezekiah Jellytop (a gentleman of large expectations and of mind soon to be)		J. G. Shain.
Stubbs (a retired Sergeant)		J. Brown.
Angelina Cockles		P. D. Butt.

God Save the Queen.

The earliest surviving playbill from the Exmoor Old Vic. Calvert and Shain were masters, and obviously busy ones. There may well have been more staff involved.

This playbill authenticates the photograph below. With a second offering as well, the audience certainly got its money's worth.

A fine testimony to the hard work that staff put in, both inside and outside the classroom. Most of the first half is the work of two men, the Headmaster himself, and his chief assistant, Thomas. And I would bet that one of them coached the choir as well. In the second half, Shain too was a master.

The famous pound-of-flesh scene from *The Merchant of Venice*, the earliest drama photo in the Archive. R.P. Chope, who played Shylock, presented this picture to the School in 1908, the year of the Jubilee. Note that Chope also had the energy left to play John Buttercup in the second play.

Harries was crazy about Gilbert and Sullivan, and was the driving force behind nearly twenty years of G. and S. productions at the School. Whatever the artistic level may have been, it is a tremendous tribute to his energy and to the joint efforts of a large proportion of the School that a small and remote academy like WB could put on such a show. This was *The Yeomen of the Guard*, from 1917, with Harries prominent, naturally, as a Beefeater.

A production of *The Gondoliers*, from December, 1926. R.F. Delderfield played the part of Inez, and appears here seated third from the right, second row from the bottom, dressed as an old woman.

This looks like a production of R.F. Delderfield's hit play *Worm's Eye View,* which made his reputation just after the Second War. The play was produced by H.A. Boyer ('Romeo'), who was Delderfield's contemporary at W.B., and who later served on the staff. Delderfield, naturally, was invited to see it. He wrote, very generously, afterwards: 'I have seldom enjoyed an evening so much. That goes for my wife too. Both of us have yawned our way through the play countless times. We know every move, every cough... but this time, it was different... The production was a great credit to Mr Boyer, his cast and his stage team... the play had a freshness and vitality that it has lacked on some previous occasions. I was very touched by the wonderful ovation the school gave me.'

What looks like a scene from *Charley's Aunt.*

Reading the will from *The Devil's Disciple.* It looks as if the family solicitor is trying too hard to steal the scene.

A young visitor to the town of Hamelin, in 1998.

❖ WHAT IS A LEAVER? ❖

Archivists inevitably come across lists – lots of them. Lists of new boys; lists of Old Boys; more recently, lists of new, and old, girls. In the older magazines, there were interminable lists of pupils who had entered for the Oxford and Cambridge Local Examinations, who had passed in First Class, Second Class, Third Class, or whatever. The first Headmaster, the Revd Thompson, was fond of recording all the names of boys who had never been late, or who had never had a complaint registered against them. Prizewinner lists figure pretty prominently, right up to the 1990s. For many years, lists of actual prizes were recorded too. Sadly, there are the lists of those Old Boys who did not come back from two World Wars. As the twentieth century advanced, the lists lengthened of pupils who had done well in an increasingly wide range of representative sport; as the School's academic reputation grew, so the lists of those who went on to university were extended.

The Sixth Form became so large at last that it became customary to publish a list of those who had left from the Upper Sixth alone. Looking at the shining faces of larger and larger groups, one came to wonder whether there was any common factor between them. Could one work out a definition? In short, what is a leaver?

For the sake of convenience, but only for the sake of convenience, and intending no offence, I shall refer to this creature from now on as 'he', although, as we all know, this creature is a human being of mixed sex.

A leaver is an animate – well, usually animate – creature of about eighteen years of age, who has spent nearly half his life in secondary schooling without becoming acquainted with education. Indeed the adolescent's resilience to education over a prolonged period is such that he could easily serve as a model to secret agents who wish to prepare themselves for severe brain-washing in the unfortunate event of their being captured by totalitarian regimes. Any human creature who has stood up with such disdainful ease to the chivvying, criticisms, pleadings, sermons, dire threats and gloomy forecasts of a whole common room full of teachers could easily take on the combined persuasive resources of the K.G.B., the *Deuxième Bureau*, and the Spanish Inquisition.

Apart from resilience, what are a leaver's chief qualities? A leaver displays loyalty – only to sedition; he displays energy – only in his pursuit of idleness; he displays passion – only in his love of apathy. What time he can spare from the abuse of his leisure he devotes to the avoidance of his studies. His greatest consistency lies in the speed with which he adopts bad habits. He will gravitate with predictable and unstoppable ease to the lowest common denominator, the worst possible taste, and the most abysmal cultural ephemera.

What are his likes and dislikes?

He is fond of undone ties, naked shirt tails, hair which impedes the eyesight, twiddling strands of hair round the fingers, and sitting in back seats in classrooms. He adores anything which is too short, too long, too tight, too loose, too cheap, or too expensive, and rings in impractical or unmentionable places. He is a sucker for novelty, romance, platforms, soap operas, rumour and gossip. He is fascinated by rebellion, protest, insubordination, smart answers, heckling, laughing in wrong places, unconventionality, tales of excess of whatever kind, and anything which is forbidden.

He can be consumed at various times by global warming, whales, badgers, stags, cloning sheep, fibre, cholesterol, red meat, live transport of animals, rain forests, *in vitro* fertilisation, refugees and genetic engineering.

He has little time for rules, conformity, current affairs, early rising, sensible eating, teetotalism, good advice, older people's reminiscences, or sitting in exam. rooms when he has finished.

His family life is a perpetual misery: he is baffled and embarrassed by babies; he is infuriated by younger brothers and sisters; he is bored by and ashamed of relations; and he is driven to despair by parents.

He is terrified of embarrassment, failure, not fitting in, exhibiting frailty, letting parents down, lines, wrinkles, old age, and anything which requires artificial support.

Does that mean that he is getting everything wrong? Quite probably. But – and this is the point – it is surely much better to get everything wrong at the start of one's life than half way through it, or, worse, at the end of it. There is so much more time to put it right. And I have so far omitted to mention one other outstanding characteristic of this creature of mixed sex – youth. It is this youth which makes the world forgive him; it is youth which makes the world hold out great hopes for him; it is youth which insulates him against his own ignorance and against the huge odds before him. It is youth which gives him the energy to attack the world, to pit himself against the minefield of troubles which the world presents – until in the end his fund of youth runs out, and he too will turn to look at the next generation coming along behind him, and he will shake his head at their innocence and ignorance and apparent vulnerability.

And – as he leaves his school and turns to face that world – what does he look forward to in the next few years? He looks forward to: systematic abuse of the body by endless participation in violent games; dedication to alcohol; burning the candle at both ends – and in the middle as well if he can manage it; travel in unsavoury parts of the world; wild excess of every conceivable kind; and carrying on generally.

One can only cling to the forlorn hope that his will be the first generation in the history of the world to wake up to the dangers of their behaviour before the arrival of the chronic tension, nervous tics, fallen arches, weak ankles, torn cartilages, slipped discs, cellulite, smoker's cough, fatty secretion, sags, scrags, bags, paunches, piles, hernias, and halitosis which characterise those who have gone before them.

In order that we may warn the world what sort of creature is going shortly to be set loose upon it, it might be as well to compose a leaver's report – which might perhaps be posted on the Internet…

Name – unknown – he forgot to put it on the exam. paper.

Date of birth – yesterday.

Sex – mixed/confused/obsessive.

Parents – two (marital status of whom is frequently open to doubt).

English – monosyllabic – thinks a sentence is what you do in prison.

Maths and Physics – can cope with Einstein, but can not add up in his head.

Chemistry – capable of blowing up the laboratory, but cannot find a kitchen cure for indigestion.

Biology – poor soul, he is a constant prey to the pressures of it.

Music – has instinctive grasp of body gyration, but cannot recognise a minim.

History – has a deep contempt for anything earlier than last week, and is convinced that senility begins at twenty-three.

Geography – can barely negotiate the London Underground.

Modern Language – fluent in the latest chat-show vernacular, but thinks a circonflex is a piece of wire used in a Jewish infant religious ceremony.

General Studies – cannot for the life of him see the point of it.

General Remarks. There are several possibilities here.

Firstly, the euphemistic. 'A charmingly relaxed attitude' – which means he is an obsequious loafer. 'Anxious to improve his performance' – which means that he's a pettifogging pedant who is always to grub up an extra mark or two on his homework.

Secondly, the quotable. 'It would be difficult to claim that he is an industrious pupil' – and leave it to the pupil to select which half to use in his C.V.

Or again, the mystified report, which one writes on the persistent absentee: 'Who is this boy?'

These days the politically correct report may have an attractive vogue. 'Motivationally challenged by virtue of negatively positive study attitude, exacerbated by compulsive screen-obsessive syndrome' – which means he does damn all work because he is glued to the box.

Then there is the jargon-riddled report (useful for those young teachers who wish to advance their career by seeking a new job in a teachers' training college or department of education). 'Levels of cognitive awareness and ratiocination temporarily stabilised in an inhibiting pre-adolescent complex of momomania for pre-pubertal preferences.' He has the mind of a ten-year-old and reads little but comics.

And, finally, there is the one for those teachers who wish to protect themselves from any come-back from pupils, parents, counsellors, social services, racial equality bureaux, left-wing journals, and the tabloid press. 'While I should not be unwilling actually to prognosticate a totally positive outcome to the forthcoming assessments of the knowledge he has fitfully and imperfectly absorbed during the last twenty months, I should not be entirely honest if I did not point out that this negative approach which he is not unwilling to demonstrate on infrequent occasions could, if circumstances were to produce an unwelcome coincidence of unexpected challenges, lead to a not entirely unexpected shortfall between desired and actual performance.' Which means – bright, but practically inert. He might pass; he might not. I'm damned if I know.

Of course, if we wish to end it all, we can throw caution to the winds and write what we really think:

'This pupil has the obstinacy and stolidity of an ox, and will probably be turned one day – and deservedly – into Bovril.'

Or – 'I am totally free from any form of prejudice; I find all my pupils equally stupid.'

And – 'Nobody could have a higher opinion of this pupil than I have – and I think he's a lazy little toad.'

But – in the 'Overall Progress' square at the bottom, we have no choice but to put:

Enthusiasm – boundless

Energy – unstoppable

Desire – all-embracing (and you can take that any way you like)

Promise – infinite

Value to the world – indispensable.

What are leavers? They are what we – the School – teachers, technicians, secretaries, cooks, nurses, cleaners, mowers, sweepers, lessons, laboratories, examinations, broken rules, tall stories, scandals, traditions, trips, parties, shows, games, gossip, good days and bad days, high days and holidays – they are what we have made them. They are to a certain extent our children.

It is a common practice in France to put on their war memorials, under or above the names of the fallen, *les enfants du village*. They do not mean 'children'; they mean the lusty, brave, loyal, devoted young people who belonged there and who wanted very much to do something which would reflect credit on the place which had nurtured them, and who wished to do their best in whatever circumstances life was to place them. *Les enfants du village*. The tone is not patronising; it is tinged with fondness and pride.

Well then, these leavers are the School's children; they are what we've got and they are what we have made of them. For better or worse, they are – unavoidably, irretrievably, and ungrammatically – us.

The Leavers of 2000.

❖ SUBSCRIBERS ❖

Roger Adams, London

Nick Adams, Bath

Johnathan M. Andrew, Umberleigh, Devon

Clive Argent, Helland, Bodmin, Cornwall. 1962-9

John Armstrong, Innerleithen

D. Armstrong Smith, Limpsfield Chart, Surrey

Dr Angela Avens, Meshaw

Mark Aveston

T. Robin Bailey, Exeter

Hugh S. Bailey, Leigh-on-Sea

Mr Christian N. J. Bailey

Richard G. Baker, Bideford

Simon M. R. Baker. 1986-97 (F)

Miss Jocelyn Balment

Martin Barwise, Cambridge

Rachel Bastiaenen

G. M. Bate, Bideford

Philip Beale, London

Dr James R. Bebb, Nottingham

Eric Bell, 26 Buck Stone, Oval, Leeds, LS17 5HG

Mr Andrew C. Bell, Kings Nympton, Devon

Robert A. Bendall, Nettlecombe

Paul and Helen Berry, West Buckland

Victoria E. Bexley, Ealing

Alan M. Billyeald

Colin Blackwell, London

Peter E. J. Bolton, Blandford, Dorset

James T. Bonetta, Northam

Mr and Mrs M. Bosworth, Barnstaple, Devon

Caroline Bradley, Surrey

Robert A. Bradley, Spalding

Bill Bray, Gloucestershire

The Brewers, South Molton, Devon

Edward S. Brown, London

Derek P. Brown

T. J. Budd, Totnes

James A. Burns, Simonsbath

Mr and Mrs G. J. Butt, West Worlington, Devon

Dr C. R. Byfleet, West Buckland School

Allan Cameron, Barnstaple, Devon

Richard W. L. Carter, Barnstaple, Devon

Heather Cavenagh-Mainwaring (née Cross), Newcastle, Staffordshire

Stephen C. Collins, Biggin Hill

J. M. Connell, Callington, Cornwall

Matias Coombs, Brentwood

Kevan Cornfield, Weybridge, Surrey

Michael E. Cornish, Okehampton (52-59 C)

Capt. Kelvin R. Crocombe, Barnstaple

D. L. Cummins

John A. Curtis, Barnstaple, Devon

Jane and Terry Daly, Torrington, Devon

Tim W. Davies, Chittlehampton, Devon

Pippa L. Davies (née Smith), Barnstaple, Devon

Crispin Dawe

Julie L. Dendle Jones, Dallas, USA

Michael Dinning, Milverton

Thomas Disken, Dewsbury

Barbara Dixon, Barnstaple, Devon

Russell J. Doane, London

Gordon R. Duncan-Hughes, Combe Martin

Richard J. Duncan-Hughes, Combe Martin

Jonathan Edmunds

William H. Edwards, formerly Totnes

Mr Kevin J. Ellicott,

Colonel R. J. Felton, East Harling

Lt Col Richard James Felton, Norfolk

Major R.F.P. Felton MBE. AAC., Ipswich

Martin D. C. Flook, Warsash

Mr Lucerne H. R. Fowler, The Devon Aire, Exeter

Mr and Mrs Arthur Fowler, Adrian, Tracey and Chantal, The Devon Aire

D. P. Freeman MBE, Bristol

John N.L. Fry, Instow

Dr Anne V. Fuchs, Munich, Germany

Tim Gardener, Chittlehampton, Devon

Mr Ian T. Gear, Newton Tracey, Devon

K. J. R. Gillies, Cheshunt

Michael C. Glen, Shrivenham

Dominic H. Gray, Edinburgh

Peter Greenway, London

Ian R. Hann, Exeter, Devon

Michael Hannaford, Aylesbury

Graham G. Harrison, Barnstaple

Tim S. Haslett, Sydney, Australia

Ben D. Haslett, Frankfurt

Mr Terence P. Hatton, Barnstaple, Devon

William R. Hawkins, West Buckland

Catherine E. Hawkins, West Buckland
A. W. Hawkins, West Buckland
Mr Nicholas W. R. Hayward, Bideford, Devon
Yvonne Helicon, Barnstaple, Devon
Phill Henshaw, Gloucester
Nicholas J. Higman, St Albans
Sydney Hillman, Barnstaple, Devon
T. K. Hitchins, Plymouth
Alan Hobbs, Solihull
Louise E. Hodgson, Bideford
Stephanie Holt, Wrafton
Sanne Holt, Wrafton
David M. Holt
Derek and Elizabeth Holt,
Matthew G. S. Hopson, Penzance
Lois Hunt, Bideford, Devon
Peter Hunt, St Alban's
Major (Ret'd) John Hyslop
William Isaac
Mr and Mrs A. G. Isaac, Kings Nympton, Devon
Ian Jackson, Crondall, Hampshire
Geoffrey Jackson, Chipping Campden
Mr Stephen M. Jackson, Zeals
'Fred', Andrew Jenkins, Bradford-on-Avon
'Fred', James Jenkins, Speen
Russell Jennings, South Molton
Adam Jennings, Angarrack
Mr T. C. Jones, Barnstaple, Devon
David J. Jones, Isle of Man
Ben Jones, Okehampton, Devon
David Joslin, Torrington
Gavin J. Keegan. 67, West Buckland 1951-1957
C. R. Keeling, Bethersden, Kent
Master Timothy Miles Keeling, Hampshire
Master Geoffrey William Keeling, Hampshire
Mrs Sarah C. Kennedy, South Molton, Devon
Edward Kent, West Buckland
Ian Kilminster, Swindon
Karim Kinani, Research Engineer, Finland
Mr Miles L. Kingsberry, Bath
Mr Dominic C. Knill, Barnstaple, Devon
Susan J. Lau, Barnstaple, Devon
Bryan Laurie, Wokingham
Steve Longmuir, Lincoln
Mark J. Loosemore, Barnstaple, Devon
Mr and Mrs J. Lovering, Combe Martin
Douglas Ludlow, Tunbridge Wells
Robert G. Maddock, Isles of Scilly
Guy M. B. Mant, London
Simon B. May, Cornwall/London

Kit and Heather Mayers, Instow
Mr Tim McMath, Horsham
John Minns, Shinfield
Peter G. Minns, Romsey
Adrian Morrey, Dorchester
Rachel Morris (nee Smith) and Stuart Morris,
    Barnstaple, Devon
Peter Morrison, Barnstaple
Morag E. Murphy, Oxford
Mark F. C. Nicholson, Gloucester
Tanith A. Nixon, Braunton, Devon
Captain T. E. Nixon
Andrew G. Nixon, Bristol
Claire and Jonathan Nutt
Duncan Oldreive
Paul Orchard-Lisle, London
A.E. Orchard-Lisle CBE (Decd.)
M. G. Orchard-Lisle MBE, France
Victoria A. Ousley, Bideford, Devon
Alan Parker, Virginia Water
E. John Parker, West Buckland
Rahul M. Patel, Barnstaple
Sir Idris Pearce
Maurice Peck, South Molton, Devon
C. Roy Penny, Bath
C. M. 'Buzz' Petherick
Robert Charles Phelps, Newport
Chris Phillips, Richmond, Surrey
Mr Brian G. J. Pile, Leicester
Mr Damian H. Pink
Dr Ian E. Pinwill, Singapore
Chris Ponder, West Buckland School
Nicola J. Portman (née Harding), Tetbury
Flt Lt C. F. Pote, Braunton
Mark and Sarah Poyner, Bideford, Devon
Cecilia Prior, Exeter (daughter – Hugh Norton-
    Pearce)
Ian Provis, Blandford
Mr David Rawle, South Molton, Devon
Michael W. H. Richards, Bath
Katy Roberts, Barnstaple
David Rooney
Nicholas Ross-Brookbank, Bristol
Rachel Rowe, Filleigh
Henry W. B. Scott, Wisbech
Ian Seager, West Buckland School
Mark A. Sellars, Brompton-on-Swale
Mrs L. H. Senn, Combe Martin, Devon
Martin K. F. Seymour, Barnstaple, Devon
Nigel Shave, Doune, Scotland

F. T. Shooter, Truro, Cornwall
Robert E. Shutler, Barnstaple
Frank Slann, Alton, Hants
Mr Michael J. R. Sluman, Barnstaple, Devon
Stuart E. M. Smith, Bratton Fleming
Peter Southcombe
A. W. Stanbury, Torquay, Devon
C.R.A.L. Start, Tavistock, Devon
David M. Stevens, Exeter (grandson – Hugh Norton-Pearce)
Kawin Surapanpitak, Bangkok
Alistair Swaine, Brisbane, Australia
Peter M. Swaine, Birmingham
David J. Terrett, Wiltshire
David A. Thair, Payhembury, Devon
George M. P. Thompson, Axminster
John Thorne, Wolverhampton
Jonathan P. A. Thornhill, Paris Texas
The Thornhills, 1967-96
John Thorpe, Clun, Shrops.
Caroline Tibble
Michael R. Tincler, Plymouth
Vice Admiral Tippet, W. Yorkshire
Arthur H. Tovey, Newport
Michael J. Tucker
Chris C. U'ren, Plymouth
R. M. Van Dissel
Mr Denis J. L. Vian
John F. Vick, West Buckland School

Douglas Vickers
John F. W. Walling, Newton Abbot, Devon
Mr David Ward, Torquay, Devon
John Watts, 1940-44
Ronald G. Way, Sidmouth, Devon
Caroline Way (née Hillman), Barnstaple, Devon
Charles Welchman, London SW11
R. J. Westacott Esq., BA Devon
Ron White, Penzance
John Whitfield, West Buckland
Richard Whitley
M. H. Wightman ('Sam'), Swindon
John Wilford, Chawleigh, Devon
Ruth Wilford, Chawleigh, Devon
Nicola, James, Lorna and Robert Wilson
Mr and Mrs G. W. Wiltshire
Mr Andrew Windsor, Barnstaple, Devon
Eric Withecombe, Woodbury, Devon
Colin C. Withecombe, Fremington
Darren and Rachel Withecombe, Middle Hearson, Swimbridge, Devon
Robert Withey, Stroud, Glos.
David N. Wolfenden
David J. P. Woodland, Taunton
Brian Woodman, Tiverton, Devon
Jonathan Woodrow, London
Michael Woodrow, Plymouth
Mrs J. P. Youings, Braunton, Devon
William F. J. R. Young, Bideford, Devon